BBQ ECON-OMICS

The content of this book is for informational purposes only and does not constitute financial advice or take your personal circumstances into account. If this is what you require, please seek the advice of a trusted financial professional.

PENGUIN

UK | USA | Canada | Ireland | Australia
India | New Zealand | South Africa | China

Penguin is an imprint of the Penguin Random House group of companies, whose addresses can be found at global.penguinrandomhouse.com.

Penguin
Random House
New Zealand

First published by Penguin Random House New Zealand, 2024

10 9 8 7 6 5 4 3 2 1

Text © Liam Dann, 2024

The moral right of the author has been asserted.

Cover design by Gemma Parmentier, based on a concept by Anns Taylor
© Penguin Random House New Zealand
Text design by Cat Taylor © Penguin Random House New Zealand
Cover illustrations by Ross Murray
Author photograph by Eleanor Dann
Prepress by Soar Communications Group
Printed and bound in Australia by Griffin Press, an Accredited ISO AS/NZS 14001 Environmental Management Systems Printer

A catalogue record for this book is available from the National Library of New Zealand.

ISBN 978-1-77695-076-8
eISBN 978-1-77695-385-1

penguin.co.nz

BBQ ECONOMICS

LIAM DANN

For Marg and Russ (Mum and Dad).
With love to Jenn, Ellie, Theo and Casey.

Contents

Introduction:

The BBQ questions

I am not an economist. That's important to know. I'm a journalist. Specifically, a business journalist who, for the past 25 years, has written about money for a living — what it is, why it matters, how it works and what it might be about to do next.

After you've been a business journalist for a while, people start asking you questions about money and that feels pretty bloody weird at first. Money can be an overly familiar topic for a casual conversation, especially for typically reserved Kiwis. Opening up about your personal finances can expose your vulnerabilities and fears. So, when friends and acquaintances start asking you about it at parties and BBQs, it can be a bit daunting. Especially if you're still standing around the brazier at 2 am.

Some of the best conversations I have still happen around that brazier. It started out with the 'boomer generation' mums and dads. Nowadays, I get a lot more questions from my peers and the younger generation too: mortgages, children, retirement savings, the price of everything from cheese to petrol to university; all these things make you pay more attention to the economic world around you.

We could choose not to pay attention to interest rates and GDP growth and just take the economic world as it comes at us. But at some point, many of us decide we want to worry about the economy. It can feel empowering and reassuring to have some context about what is going on. In fact, one of the questions I'm asked most often is: How worried should we be about it all? I always reply: How worried do you want to be?

If you like to worry, then economics has you covered. It draws from an almost infinite pool of doom and gloom. It is a famously pessimistic discipline. In the 19th century, it was dubbed 'the dismal science' by Scottish writer Thomas Carlyle, in response to the grim predictions of population collapse made by his buddy Thomas Malthus. Carlyle also described economics as 'dreary, desolate and, indeed, quite abject and distressing'.

It says something about human nature that it's still such a popular topic. If anything, it's more popular than ever. We have celebrity economists now, media stars who predict the future or confirm our suspicions about the world – or confound them. We live-stream Reserve Bank press conferences and debate inflation and interest rates and recession risk on social media. We wonder about how to improve productivity and make the country a wealthier place. And then we stand around the work coffee machine, or at the parties or that BBQ and we try to work it all out.

I get asked about recession risks and share market crashes and cryptocurrency. I get asked about bank profits, high-rolling wheeler-dealers and the threat of robots taking our jobs. Most of the time, though, the questions are about mortgage rates or house prices – or both. Let's face it, for Kiwis, when it comes to finance, property is where the rubber hits the road. Should I fix or float? Is now a good time to buy – or sell? How does the Official Cash Rate actually work? Or it's the economics of daily life: Why does cheese cost so much when we make so much of the stuff? Is Australia really much richer than New Zealand? And why? Why are Kiwis so far behind the rest of the world in productivity. And what does productivity even mean?

In this book, I'm going to try and answer some of these classic Kiwi BBQ questions. If you just want to feel less anxious about money – if you want to know why things go up and why things go down, if you want to understand the forces that shape your financial life – then I hope the stuff here helps. If you just want to sound smarter at BBQs when talk turns to interest rates, then *BBQ Economics* has you covered. It's packed full of the intel that has helped me during my career in the thick of it all. If you want to understand what makes Aotearoa New Zealand different, and how we got where we are today, then this is the book for you, too. More importantly, though, I hope it's going to help you see that economics isn't really so hard.

On one level, economics is just contemplating money. And we all think about money every day – even if it's just that we'd like some of more of it. We think about paying our bills, we think about saving for our retirement, or for a holiday. We think about what that drunken bender did to our credit card balance on Friday night. We dream about winning Lotto, we imagine being rich, we worry about being poor. Economics is thinking about money and all the things that money represents. It's thinking about the value of things: resources, needs, wants and luxuries. What value do we put on our time and labour? How do we measure success? Does more wealth mean more happiness?

Economics puts a price on deep human desires. It puts a price on risk and a price on security. It goes to the heart of our thoughts about social inequality and fairness ... and it's always political. We seldom agree on our goals as a society – let alone how we should reach them – so it's not surprising that we never agree about this economics stuff.

Economists agree broadly on quite a lot, although they seem to never quite agree, exactly, on anything. Of course, some economists are believers in ideology – from the left and the right – with wildly divergent views about human history, psychology and behaviour as their starting points.

(We'll look at all that in this book and how those beliefs have shaped New Zealand.) But economics also helps us to clarify the choices we can make, as individuals and collectively. Money shapes the world, and thinking a bit more about it might even help us make that world a better place.

It's also fun. Or at least it can be fun if we're thinking about it because we want to, as opposed to because we have to. For many of us, economics was just that class you took in the sixth form because your parents thought you should learn about money and accounting was just too boring to cope with. Unfortunately, sometimes, for some reason, when we label all that interesting money-stuff 'economics', people can find it daunting. Economics does have its own language. But so do hip-hop, cricket, gardening or any number of other (fun!) pastimes.

Economics can be dry. In fact, for many decades it was deliberately so. There was an elitism that seemed designed to maintain exclusivity about the knowledge. That has created an aura about economics, a myth that understanding it offers some secret key to the rich-list. Let's say it upfront: reading this book won't make you rich. Although, if you really, really want to get rich, then it might help. And it can't hurt. It could certainly help you to avoid being poor. I've included insights and advice from dozens of the super-smart economists, finance gurus, CEOs, political leaders and rich-listers I've been lucky to talk to and learn from over the years — some of which might surprise you.

Like I said at the start, I'm a journalist, not an economist — and that's important. I try to be unbiased when I explain economic concepts — especially the political bits. I see value in ideas from the left and the right — although seldom at the extremes. My version of economics, like yours, is informed by my personal experiences, and this book is my view on a world I've been privileged to be a part of, professionally, for a quarter of a century. So when I write about inflation, it reflects childhood and teenage memories of the endlessly spiralling cost of living through the late 1970s and '80s. When I write about unemployment, it is with the experience of leaving university in 1992 — with the national unemployment rate at 12 per cent. When I write about the Global Financial Crisis it is coloured by my experiences covering it as a young journalist.

Our lives inevitably shape our views — which is just a fancy way of saying that readers — expert, armchair and everyone in between — should feel free to disagree with mine. That's all part of what I love about economics — especially *BBQ Economics*. I hope you enjoy it.

Chapter 1

Money
stories

Whoever tells the best story wins.
— John Quincy Adams

....

I t was a dark and stormy night.

No, really, it was.

It was early evening on a weekend in late July 2008. Auckland's politicians and business leaders were gathered in the conference room of the War Memorial Museum to hear an address by the visiting US secretary of state, Condoleezza Rice.

The wind and rain lashed the large window panes, but Auckland's high society had dressed up and braved the weather. I remember thinking that all that was needed to complete the picture was the Joker to arrive and Batman to come crashing through the ceiling. Rice gave her speech and nothing quite so dramatic as a superhero battle unfolded.

But actually, there was something big happening around us. A worrying rumour was sweeping the room. The night sticks in my mind because it was when I realised that the Global Financial Crisis was going to change our lives. In the *Business Herald* we'd been covering the credit crunch since the previous year, but the meltdown building through 2008 was yet to make the leap to the general news.

For most people, the full scale of the GFC didn't really hit until the collapse of the investment bankers Lehman Brothers on 12 September that year. But that dark winter evening at the museum is the first time I felt emotionally connected to the thing, and aware of its enormity.

It meant people were going to lose their jobs, businesses would fail, lives would be turned upside down, the course of history was going to change.

I felt real fear and even some mild panic at the prospect that New Zealand's economy was about to take a monumental blow. Everyone in the room that night was feeling it. The story circulating over champagne and bacon-wrapped scallops was that one of the big Aussie banks was in trouble, embroiled somehow in the complex mess of financial derivatives that was shaking the US economy. Were the dominoes of the GFC falling our way?

Spoiler alert: they weren't. At least, not yet.

World on the brink

It's easy to forget, but there was a moment when the GFC threatened to bring the entire global economy to a grinding halt.

Three of Wall Street's top five independent investment banks were wiped out. All three — Bear Stearns, Lehman Brothers and Merrill Lynch — pre-dated the crash of 1929. They had survived the Great Depression and the 1987 crash, but not 2008.

In the same week in September that Lehman Brothers went down, the US government bailed out global insurance giant AIG to the tune of US$85 billion. It was feared that its failure would cause a meltdown of the worldwide insurance sector. Without insurance, airlines would have to ground their planes.

'If any doubt was left, events of the past two days have shunted the gravity of the US financial meltdown past that of the Black Monday crash in October 1987. Pundits are now making comparisons with the big collapse of 1929, which caused the Great Depression.' I wrote those words for an editorial that ran on the front page of the *Herald* on 17 September 2008.

By that point it felt like I was shouting at New Zealanders to pay attention to the scale of what was coming at them. High drama on Wall Street can seem exciting but distant from this little island at the far end of the world, but we are unavoidably connected to the global economy, with all its upsides and downsides.

In the end, the GFC did all sorts of damage to the New Zealand economy, but it didn't come close to the Great Depression. Our world kept turning — just. Unemployment leapt from 3.6 per cent at the end of 2007 to 6.1 per cent by the end of 2010, but the central banks, having learned from history, made bold calls that meant nobody had to go and plant trees on government work schemes.

In fact, while it was more dramatic on a global scale, the GFC wasn't as damaging as the series of recessions New Zealand experienced between 1987 and 1994. (Of course, that might depend on how old you were at the time, whether you had a secure job or how much debt you had.) Nonetheless, the GFC is going to loom large in my story. The crisis and the narrative around it shaped a lot of my thoughts about finance and economics because I was young and suddenly found myself in the thick of it.

Telling stories

Stories are powerful things. They can be dangerous. In fact, they are considered so dangerous in financial situations that we have strict laws in place about them. The economic and financial world exists in a sea of rumours, stories and narratives. The system floats along on them.

These stories can be very specific, like inside information about an impending takeover offer, or speculation about a bank collapse. They can be short and sharp, causing a panicked share market crash or a bubble of investment mania. Or they can be slow-burning: ideas about new ways to make money, to get rich and beat the system, infecting the popular psyche until they become the dominant world view — affecting our behaviour and the way we make policies to run the world. They gather momentum until they become such a dominant narrative in the culture that their merits or underlying truth are barely questioned. And then they collapse. And when they do that, they usually take a lot of wealth with them.

Stories are increasingly recognised as forming a crucial part of the economic equation. In his 2019 book *Narrative Economics*, Nobel Memorial Prize-winning economist Robert J. Shiller makes the case for taking them seriously. 'We need to incorporate the contagion of narratives into economic theory,' he writes. 'Otherwise, we remain blind to a very real, very palpable, very important mechanism for economic change, as well as a crucial element for economic forecasting.'

In other words, the narrative isn't just the description of the events unfolding in the economy: it is an active player in those events.

We need to recognise stories as they catch hold, and contextualise them quickly, if we hope to make sense of the economic world. They're uniquely human, which means they are often unpredictable. And telling stories is where journalists like me enter the equation. So that seems like a good place to start on the journey towards making sense of the modern economy — with stories.

Economic and investment market narratives aren't so different from the ebb and flow of fashion, art and music. New styles emerge into the popular consciousness with the help of storytellers. Often — and especially in finance, economics and business — the real value lies in getting in on a trend early. By the time everyone knows the story, it is usually past its use-by date, and the smart money is already getting out; cutting and running.

If the media is doing its job, it is informing people that the tale is done. In that respect, the Global Financial Crisis is perhaps a controversial example if we're going to talk about the media's role as a watchdog of the economic narrative. After all, it's been said we didn't do a great job of warning the public. But the GFC was a like a slow-motion train wreck. By the time we were sure it was happening, it was too late.

Regardless, if journalists play any significant role in the economy, that role is in the narratives that shape it. So let's look at how those narratives are shaped.

Shoeshine boys and tulip bubbles

Like many people, Joseph Kennedy (President JFK's dad) had great success investing on Wall Street through the Roaring Twenties. Unlike a lot of people, he was able to realise that wealth by getting out of the market shortly before the big crash in 1929.

The story has it that Kennedy Snr stopped in the street one day to get his shoes polished and was taken aback when the kid with the brushes began offering hot stock market tips. Kennedy took that as a sign that the bubble was about to burst and got out of the market. Like a lot of good stories, it may not have actually happened, but that doesn't matter. It's a story that rings so true that it continues to be told. Perhaps it's a hairdresser in 1987 telling you to get in on the float of an angora goat farm. Or it's the guy at the video store tipping you off about hot tech stock in 1999. Or your Uber driver yesterday telling you which cryptocurrency you need to buy.

In all its forms, the moral of this story is that by the time it's being told by an ordinary bloke in the street, there's an investment bubble and it's about to pop. That's a pretty cynical outlook, but it does reflect the reality that early access to these stories (and the safer, more lucrative end of an investment boom) is exclusive and confers power and advantage. If you are among the first to see the financial advantage in a new narrative, you'll make money. If you are first to see a crash coming, you'll avoid losing money.

In the Dutch Golden Age, the warning sign might have been an alchemist or blacksmith telling you which tulip bulb would be the next big thing. The tulip bubble of the 1630s is one of my favourite cautionary financial tales. It's often described as a mania, a mass public delusion.

Tulip bulbs were a status symbol in seventeenth-century Europe, and certain varieties developed by Dutch growers were so rare that bulbs were traded for values exceeding the annual salary of a craftsman, or, in one legendary case, five times the value of a house. A good bulb could flower and generate several more bulbs, so the investment was sure to pay off as long as the price kept rising. It didn't, of course.

There was a crash, which infamously took down some wealthy Dutch families, and it has served as a metaphor for unhinged market booms ever since. As usual, spoilsport academics have looked closely at the tale and now argue it was blown wildly out of proportion in the retelling. Again, that hardly matters. It's an excellent example of market values becoming unhinged from any real-world value — something that happens time and time again in the investment world. It is also a reminder that stories don't have to be true to change the world.

On that night in the museum back in 2008, the rumour wasn't true. At least, it mostly wasn't. The big Aussie banks weren't really in trouble. In the final wash-up, just one — ANZ, through its investment division — had exposure to the arcane products (collateralised debt options) that were at the heart of the GFC meltdown. Perhaps in the room that night people had drawn a connection to that ANZ fund — who knows? — but the fears about the local fallout from the GFC didn't abate. They hung around through the market meltdowns of the next few months and the world-shaking collapse of Lehman Brothers in September.

By October, the concern resulted in New Zealand following Australia and putting a state guarantee in place for banks and other financial institutions. That unfortunately included finance companies: second-tier lenders offering better returns than the banks. Many of them turned out to be badly run and heavily invested in risky assets. Their owners put a lot of effort into selling stories about safety and security. They also spent heavily on lawyers to prevent the media countering those stories. That government guarantee was eventually called on to cover the losses as those companies collapsed — all of them, one by one, until the entire sector was gone. It ended up costing the country about NZ$2 billion, although some of that was recovered.

Once the finance companies started collapsing, New Zealand's financial crisis narrative changed. But all of it — the whole credit crunch and subsequent financial crash — was built on contagious stories being treated as facts by the investment community. The property market always rises, mortgage derivatives are a safe investment, the banks are too big to fail: all these stories were true. Until they weren't.

As ever, there were contrarians at the time. There are always economists or financial commentators who have a pessimistic bias. And yet you only have to look at the performance of markets and economies across a long period to see that the general trend is mostly positive. Balancing optimism and pessimism in the way we tell economic stories is a constant juggling act for journalists.

What makes economics news?

The stories we tell to try and make sense of the economy usually start with data. That means numbers. Basically it's just about counting and measuring things. The good news is that if you can find the story the numbers are telling, you don't have to be good at maths. You just have to get over your fear of numbers in the first place.

We've touched on market stories already. The big share market crashes — 1929, 1987 and 2008 — tend to demand our attention because they are dramatic. We'll come back to them throughout this book. But everyday market pricing is also reported in real time for all sorts of things, from oil and food to currency and debt (the price of borrowing). Market movements might be influenced by stories, but prices are facts; they are cold, hard pieces of reality, however ridiculous they might seem. If a price is recorded somewhere, it's because two parties agreed on it; a transaction happened. At that point, we can really strip economics back to the basic law of supply and demand.

There might be weird reasons for any one sale price. A seller might be desperate, or a buyer may have some strong emotional attachment. But if we record all the transactions on a market in a day or a week (or even a minute) and average them, we get a pretty solid idea of the current market value of something. Those prices have an immediate impact on our economic lives: the weekly grocery shopping, a tank of petrol, our mortgage payments, and even how much we earn.

When it comes to daily economic news, some markets are more interesting than others. The markets most closely covered are those that go to the heart of an economic system and influence the price of everything else. The price of a particular currency — relative to another — provides a constant flow of stories all around the world. On currency markets something like US$7 trillion is traded every day in millions of individual transactions. That means you can look up the market data on any two currencies and watch the price move in real time.

The way a currency's value moves almost always tells some sort of economic story. If we see the Kiwi dollar is falling in value against the US dollar, we know something's happening. Maybe there was some good news in the US, or bad news in New Zealand. I once watched with my heart in my mouth as the Kiwi dollar plunged drastically on speculation that New Zealand's dairy herd had an outbreak of foot-and-mouth disease (it didn't, and the dollar bounced back immediately).

Currency traders are highly reactive, and they don't muck around. There's a lot of 'trusting your gut'. Former New Zealand prime minister Sir John Key, once a highly successful currency trader, told me it was an art, not a science. I think it was Key's ability to get to the heart of a narrative that made him so good at politics and good at market trading — he was highly skilled at picking up on stories, seeing which way they were unfolding and backing the winners. I'll share some of his advice on money later on when we look at investing.

It's stories that drive currency markets and determine what a Kiwi dollar is worth. In other words, they define (in pure financial terms) what we are worth as a nation. They shape all the big commodity markets, especially oil markets. If the price of oil rises or falls sharply, then there must be a story behind it. Those stories are often complex geopolitical tales, but they flow through to the price of getting the kids to football practice. It might be war and strife in the Middle East or US sanctions on Iran or an edict from the Chinese government. Oil markets still have a huge influence on the global economy.

There's plenty more to say about oil and markets and pricing. For now, let's just accept that markets give us data that fuels our economic storytelling.

SUPPLY AND DEMAND

The law of supply and demand flows through economics like the Force flows through the *Star Wars* universe. It's deep and fundamental: its energy surrounds us and binds us, as Yoda liked to say.

Okay: technically, supply and demand are two forces, and there's one law about how they interact. And yes, it may also be a bit soon to be pulling out a *Star Wars* analogy, given how many of these explainers lie ahead. But if I get to use just one in this book, then it belongs here. That's how important supply and demand are.

Supply and demand keep the economic universe in balance. They underpin economic interactions. In that sense, they've been with us as long as we've been economic animals. 'Everything is worth what its purchaser will pay for it,' wrote the philosopher Publilius Syrus in the first century BCE. Syrus spoke from experience, having arrived in Rome from Syria as a slave.

Supply and demand (the term itself was coined in the eighteenth century) is almost a law of nature, and about as solid as laws get in economics. It describes the relationship between the quantity of something people want (demand) and the quantity that's available (supply). It predicts that if demand is higher than supply, the price of something will rise. If supply is higher than demand, then the price will fall.

Economists plot this relationship on a graph, with price on the vertical axis and quantity along the base. The demand curve generally runs downward from left to right, indicating that as the price (vertical axis) decreases, the quantity demanded (horizontal axis) rises, and vice versa.

The supply curve slopes upward from left to right and shows that as the price increases, the quantity supplied also increases (and as quantity supplied decreases the price rises).

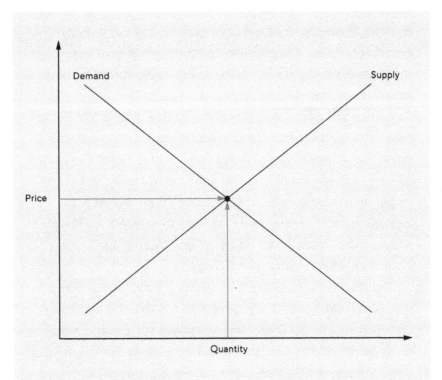

So far, so good.

Now, we add human motivation to get the best deal — something the philosopher and economist Adam Smith dubbed 'the invisible hand'. When prices for something — cheese, say — are high, people will be motivated to produce more of it and the quantity available should rise, exerting downward pressure on the price. When cheese prices are low, there is less motivation to produce it (dairy companies might as well just sell milk powder). Supply dwindles, and that creates upward price pressure. Those two opposing forces create a tension, which pushes supply one way and demand the other until the two curves meet. That point is the market price. Bingo! We have a deal.

This is not just a point in an economist's notebook. In the real world it is where two parties decide the price is right. It's not an arbitrary point based on fair value, either, as it doesn't necessarily reflect the effort and resources that went into making something. It simply indicates what the price is when supply meets demand.

Supply and demand is a law that makes a mockery of all the time, effort and expensive ingredients you put into your kid's school bake sale. If no one wants your organic carrot and kale muffins (if they want the off-the-shelf brandy snaps bought by another, lazier parent), then it doesn't matter what your ingredients cost or how hard they were to bake. So the law of supply and demand is not warm or fuzzy, like a grand human ideal. It's cold and brutal, like biology.

There's plenty more to say about supply and demand and the human behaviour that moves both around, and about how prices change under those different pressures. But that's as far as we need to go with this *Star Wars* analogy. The Force got less fun when George Lucas started explaining it with Midichlorians and whatnot. For now, let's just accept you are going to have to sell those muffins below cost.

Chapter 2

What even is money?

All money is a matter of belief.
— Adam Smith

....

The idea that competition for economic resources is the basis for much of the conflict in the world is a no-brainer. Scarcity of resources is what makes economics important. It's also what makes it controversial.

But although people have argued about money throughout history, we haven't resolved whether it is good or bad. The Bible has it that the love of money is the root of all evil (pre-dating Karl Marx and his conflict theory by almost 2000 years). According to many anthropologists, however, money was fundamental in the cultural leap we took thousands of years ago to create complex societies. Money was a breakthrough on an evolutionary scale. It underpins our success as a species.

Darwin's evolutionary theory, the survival of the fittest, doesn't fit too badly with classical capitalist economics. There's a 'sink or swim' dynamic at play in the world of free enterprise. But let's not forget that money and trade also brought us a world where the fittest need no longer be the physically strongest or fastest, or even the most aggressive.

Art, as Bob Dylan argues in *The Philosophy of Modern Song*, is a disagreement: the best of it deliberately provokes and challenges. Money, on the other hand, is a device for resolving or avoiding conflict. It allows two parties to achieve their respective goals. The invention of money allowed people to agree on values with one another, even with those outside their tribal or family bonds. It was a means of accord, free of the need for emotional or social connection.

Money and economy brought opportunity to people with a wide range of skill sets. The mechanism to put a price on things enabled a world where labour could be divided and, as a result, productivity improved on an exponential scale. That enabled civilisations with surplus food, where leisure and decadence became possible. It gave humans time to contemplate the universe; the search for meaning became a commodity, and religion flourished.

In the modern world I can get on my phone and order a pair of sneakers from America and a tee-shirt from China — and, as if by magic, there is an instantly agreed price, despite all the barriers of geography, language and currency. In ancient Mesopotamia, just being able to trade my excess fruit for your excess grain made all the difference. And then being able to trade some of that grain for meat and that meat for pottery or spears, and so on. Trade built interaction outside the clan that didn't involve violence. And when that grew too complex, money was invented to keep tabs on value.

Anthropologists argue that trade via currency existed in many cultures long before (and after) the invention of coins. Shells, knotted ropes, beads and even complex oral records of credit and debt have underpinned economies in many parts of the world. But there's a rough consensus that the first coins — shekels — emerged about 5000 years ago in Mesopotamia. It was a milestone in societal evolution, enhancing the authority of the state and enabling the building of empires. Shekels talked. The idea caught on.

Money in the modern world can seem infinitely complex now. But whether it's a series of binary numbers on a digital balance sheet in the twenty-first century or a chanted song of debt and obligation in the oral culture of hunter–gatherers, it's all a ledger built on trust and shared belief. For all the moaning and complaining about commercial banks and central banks and governments, we still trust them more than we don't. If the trust fails, we know about it very quickly.

Counting sheep . . . and everything else

Governments have been collecting data about their people and resources for about as long as there have been governments. The first recorded census was some 6000 years ago in the city of Babylon, where officials counted sheep and cattle and quantities of butter, honey, milk, wool and vegetables. The records don't mention beans specifically. But somewhere along the way, someone was pedantic enough about counting beans to curse their fellow accountants with that patronising nickname for the rest of history.

Ironically, history does record the first bean counter's name – he (or she) was an ancient Sumerian called Kushim, from the fourth millennium BCE. Okay, they probably weren't the world's first accountant. But Kushim, an administrator and record keeper, has the honour of being the earliest known person to have their name recorded in writing. The name appears in a tablet record of accountants so, as *National Geographic* puts it, Kushim was 'a record keeper who counted things for others – in short, an accountant'.

I don't think that's a coincidence. It tells us something about the significance of economics in human history. Kushim didn't count beans, though. The tablets recorded the sale of barley, hops and malt – the ingredients for beer. So the story of economic data pretty much begins with someone keeping a score of how much beer the kingdom was producing. No surprises there.

Recording economic data was a breakthrough because it meant that people could then compare one year with the next. They could try and work out what was going wrong in the bad years and what was going right in the good years. Measuring production allowed people to improve their technique and produce more stuff.

Another upside, if you were the king, was it gave you an idea of the extent you could tax your people. Long before anyone decided to call this stuff economics, people were keeping tabs on economies. To rule an empire the size of Rome somebody had to be doing a lot of counting and taxing. All these centuries later, we still count sheep.

When I was growing up in New Zealand, it was a running joke (with Australians, anyway) that we were a nation of 66 million sheep and three million people. These days there are far fewer sheep. Counting cows has become a lot more important to our economy, thanks to the dairy boom. In fact, we count everything we produce in the economy, what we call the gross domestic product. GDP doesn't count work done on a voluntary basis or in the home because . . . well, actually that's a fairly controversial omission these days.

I'll look at the merits and shortcomings of GDP in more detail later, along with deep dives into the other top-tier economic data, such as inflation (price movements) and unemployment (the labour market). Those three make up the trifecta of economic statistics — the Beatles, Elvis and the Rolling Stones, if you like. That said, there are other important things we count which also offer clues to the economy — such as population, new buildings and migration levels.

As it was in ancient times, counting all this stuff is done by the state, by the Department of Statistics, better known as Stats NZ Tatauranga Aotearoa. Stats NZ publishes reports and new numbers on a monthly or quarterly basis. A couple of other important institutions collect and publish economic data. There's the Treasury Te Tai Ōhanga — effectively the state's finance division. The Treasury keeps tabs on revenue, expenditure and debt, and its big performance piece is the annual Budget. The finance minister puts that together based on the government's policies and plans and informed by advice from the Treasury.

But the Treasury also puts out updates of the government's financial performance and position every six months. Those numbers have a big impact on how the nation is rated by financial institutions internationally. That rating influences things like the value of our currency and how much it costs us to borrow. For small countries like New Zealand the government accounts matter a lot. If one of the big financial ratings agencies decides they don't look too good, it doesn't take many international currency traders to ruin our economy.

The other big institution for data is the central bank — the Reserve

Bank of New Zealand in our case, akin to the Bank of England or the US Federal Reserve. The Reserve Bank is owned by the government, although theoretically it is independent of parliamentary interference. It has the power to control the country's money supply by setting the wholesale cost of borrowing. (When it comes to economic news, events don't get much bigger than central bank decisions about interest rates.) But central banks also monitor the financial stability of the country and count the nation's private debt levels.

So, all these institutions publish numbers, along with some industry associations like the Real Estate Institute of New Zealand, which keeps tabs on house prices. The media enthusiastically republishes this data with the most interesting bits at the top, and then we argue about whether the numbers are good or bad. In fact, we usually start arguing before the numbers come out, with previews and forecasts and speculation from economists setting general expectations and the way the story will get told.

Modern soothsayers

The profile of market economists has risen steadily in the past 25 years (often amplified by the work of financial journalists like me). By market economists we really just mean the ones that work for commercial organisations, those working for major retail banks and financial investment firms — as opposed to academics with loftier longer-term outlooks. There's also a range of independent economists working for think tanks (basically business consultancies) who put out their own forecasts and reports on market data.

Telling stories about the economy is a big part of the marketing strategy for these organisations. The economists will publish regular reports, which clients and customers can access directly. But to hit a wider audience and ensure the company's brand is holding a solid spot in the public conversation, these economic reports, analyses and forecasts are widely shared with the media.

These days, when an important new piece of economic data is

published it can be quite a media circus. In the 25 years I've been covering economics, I've watched the hype grow as big number drops have been embraced as mainstream news events. In fact, I've probably played a part in building that hype. I've pushed hard over the years to get economics off the business pages and onto the front pages.

I've also spent plenty of time looking at news coverage of historic financial events. Often, I'll write anniversary articles remembering the 1987 or 1929 crashes. In 1929 the Wall Street Crash was reported as a brief in the *New Zealand Herald*. The 1987 crash was more of a mainstream media event because, by then, ordinary New Zealanders had been a lot more exposed to the share market. But Reserve Bank decisions and statistical economic data didn't get the huge spotlight on them they do now. Government budgets were bigger deals back then — reflecting the greater role of the state in our lives.

Things changed with the GFC, which was the first major meltdown of the internet age. We all have access to more information now and a lot more opinions. The trouble is we are swamped by them — both the optimistic and the pessimistic. For every article raving about a new investment boom, there's another warning that it's all going to crash. That's hopefully where journalists come in. And good market regulation.

I could complain and go on about the good old days. But rather than bemoan the hyperbolic style of the modern media, let's say that wider engagement of the public with these economic issues is a good thing. Here in the internet age, all the big economic and financial narratives are out there and available to anybody who wants to read them.

For better or worse

The way I see it, how we tell the first story about a new piece of economic data is a binary decision. Economists have already published their forecasts, and the markets have priced their expectations for where numbers (such as an interest rate hike, or inflation or GDP or unemployment) will land.

So, the first and often the most important piece of news is: was the number higher or lower than expected? Once we know that, we can extrapolate all sorts of ramifications. Any assumptions will also be confirmed – or rejected – within seconds by the market reaction.

When a big piece of data is released, we will usually have a live currency chart open on a computer terminal in the newsroom, so we can watch the market react to the data in real time. If the dollar sinks or soars, we instantly know we have a big story.

An example might be annual consumer price inflation coming in stronger than expected. Obviously, a bigger annual rise is bad news because it means we're all paying more for bread and cheese and stuff. But the data is a record of what happened in the last year (or quarter year). We've already experienced the increase, so, while the news desk will still want a headline about the price of cheese, the real story is in the economic implications of the data.

If inflation is running high, then the Reserve Bank is likely to lift interest rates to try and get it under control (higher rates reduce the money supply and cool consumer demand). If the Reserve Bank was already expected to lift the interest rate, then higher inflation will lock in those odds – perhaps prompting speculation that the rate will rise by more than planned. If, however, the Reserve Bank was expected to reduce the interest rate, then the new data may prompt it to pause.

If rates are going higher than expected, it means a bigger reduction of the money supply and the economy will likely slow by more than expected. That means companies will invest less and unemployment may rise. It means house prices may fall ... and so on.

Basically, if we stick to the classic economic formulae, there's a lot we can say very quickly after just one big number is revealed. How aggressively the media decides to go with all this extrapolation is controversial. A cynic might say we journalists manipulate the narrative. I think that ascribes too much power to us individually. We all have some degree of personal bias. Most journalists I know and work with do their best to account for that bias in news coverage and declare it in their commentary.

For the love of money

Of course, money became, and remains, a source of envy and greed and conflict. But is it really the root of all evil? Or just some of it? The full biblical verse, attributed to second-division apostle Timothy of Ephesus, isn't quite as damning of money as the shorthand version that remains popular today.

'For the love of money is the root of all evil: which while some coveted after, they have erred from the faith, and pierced themselves through with many sorrows.' (That, at least, is the King James version of 1 Timothy 6, verse 11.)

So, it isn't money that is evil, but more humanity's capacity to fall in love with the pursuit of it. Either way, Saint Timothy was clearly no fan of the personal finance industry. 'People who long to be rich fall into temptation and are trapped by many foolish desires and schemes that plunge them into ruin and destruction,' he wrote (verse 9).

Those words remain unnervingly relevant in today's world of Ponzi schemes and cryptocurrency scams. They make for a timely, if slightly depressing, reminder of how little the economic behaviour of humans has really changed.

FOMO: THE FEAR OF MISSING OUT, OR OPPORTUNITY COST

Do you suffer from FOMO — the fear of missing out? If you've ever had two competing invitations to events on the same night, then you've certainly wrestled with it. Will I have more fun going to the gig with Dave or to Gabe's BBQ? It's generally not just a simple equation: the choice to go and enjoy one event comes at the cost of not going and enjoying the other.

In economics that's called an opportunity cost. The opportunity cost represents the potential gains we might miss out on from a future investment because we invested the capital elsewhere. It is the opposite of a sunk cost (see page 221), which is a decision that has already been made and the money spent.

Assessing an opportunity cost involves looking into the future, which is always complex and imperfect. In our social lives these decisions involve lots of variables that are hard to quantify. Will all the people I want to talk to actually turn up at the BBQ? Will it be a great gig, or will the band be tired and flat?

In business and micro-economics, the opportunity cost of financial decisions is an even more pressing issue. Good decision-making around opportunity costs can even be make or break for a business. If your company makes a good profit, what's the best thing to do with the profit? Should you reinvest in the business? Should you hire more staff, upgrade your tools and equipment, or pay down debt? Should you buy your rival's business?

Some opportunity costs will be easier to see than others. If you have a good idea of how much extra profit you can generate for every extra worker you hire, then you can benchmark that rate of return against the costs you will save by paying down debt. Of course, nothing is certain: the extra worker might be lazy, or the interest rate on your debt might change.

Usually, assessing opportunity costs involves a trade-off between returns and risk. Imagine you have $100,000 to invest and you can get five per cent a year in the bank, versus an expected average return of seven per cent in a share market fund. The bank is going to give you a $5000 return, while the share market should (based on average returns across time) beat that and give you about $7000. In theory, the opportunity cost of putting the money in the bank is $2000. But the share market is riskier. There might be a crash just after you invest, and you might lose money — in the short term, at least. You might also describe that extra $2000 as a risk premium.

We can't know all the possible outcomes with certainty, but at least we can work through all the possibilities to make informed decisions.

Christianity has never resolved its relationship with money and wealth, struggling throughout history to live up to its own message. Just take a look at the opulence of the Catholic Church or the modern evangelical organisations with their unashamedly wealthy figureheads.

If anything, those moral dilemmas around money have just spilled over into our secular social systems as the power of the church has waned and that of the state has grown. To what extent should we celebrate money and embrace its pursuit? Without restraint, where does the impulse to chase money lead? Nowhere good, usually.

So, should we restrain and regulate it? But how? And how strictly? If we suppress our selfish desires too aggressively, will we kill them and, in doing so, stifle the desire to improve and enrich life? Will we end up like the Soviet Union of the twentieth century, incapable of designing fashionable denim jeans and stylish sports cars?

We call the proposed answers to these dilemmas 'politics' and then, traditionally, we put them on a linear spectrum running left to right. Then we pick a side.

Chapter 3

Adam Smith vs Karl Marx vs your angry friend on Facebook

*Politics is the art of
controlling your environment.
— Hunter S. Thompson*

....

Politics makes a right old mess of economics. It sends us around in circles, or back and forth, on social problems that look, on paper, highly surmountable. They don't say 'political enthusiast', do they? They say 'junkie'. The term evokes a tragic and painful relationship with the topic, an addiction we couldn't shake even if we wanted to.

Every year, there seems to be a new benchmark for political craziness. The British Brexit vote and the election of Donald Trump in the US made 2016 something of a landmark year for the weirdness.

And our traditional notions of political division have been distorted and confused by the culture wars that have been raging around us for decades. Are you a liberal or conservative, progressive or traditional? Are you a socialist, capitalist, neoliberal or monetarist? There is a loud and often angry discourse that's full of labels. It clouds politics and muddies economic debate.

The internet hasn't helped; social media has amplified that weirdness. We live in a 24/7 news stream of hot takes, where nothing can happen without politicisation, opinion and debate. So let's dial it back a bit and look at the age-old ideological divide around money and how we organise the economy. What is it that we are arguing about?

Who's left, who's right and who's wrong?

The popular model has it that the left strives for social equality and fairness. It sees regulation and central government as the means to ensure and enforce that. The right says, No — greed is good (or at least not all bad); the impulse to improve one's lot is natural, not selfish, and it drives humanity forwards.

In the eighteenth century, Adam Smith dubbed that driving force 'the invisible hand'. The right argues that attempts to deny this impulse are naïve at best, dangerous at worst. The right seeks to minimise government and regulation, trusting in market forces and our ability to trade our way to social equilibrium.

Most modern democracies run as a mixed model of left and right thinking, juggling and balancing these two political positions. Ideally, the tension they create gives the system flexibility and balance; but all too often, the conflict creates gridlock and inaction on important issues — which at least gives newspaper columnists plenty to write about.

Where you, as a voter, sit on that linear political spectrum from the left wing to the right can define you. If you care enough, you might base your life around your spot on that left–right axis. It might determine your job, your friends, the music you listen to and the books you read.

We humans like a dichotomy; we're fans of a binary choice. It keeps things tidy. Deep down, we know the world is more complex. But it's much harder to visualise the three-dimensional matrix that truly incorporates all the choices and variables that shape our lives.

These days, the politics of left and right are increasingly confused and complicated by the cultural divides around social issues like race, gender, abortion, climate change, and personal freedoms.

We only need look at the eclectic mix of coalition anti-lockdown, anti-vaccine protesters that converged on Parliament in 2022. It brought together right-wing libertarians and alternative lifestyle hippies in a way that would have seemed implausible before the pandemic.

People can be economically conservative and culturally liberal. Or they may be culturally conservative, but lean economically towards the state control of the left. In some respects, the values of free-market, small-state libertarianism sit better with the personal freedom advocated by cultural liberals, while socialism and state control can often lend themselves to cultural conservatism.

It's hard to make the case that Josef Stalin was a liberal lefty, or that the extreme-right fascism of Adolf Hitler made the Nazis advocates of the free market. Both of those guys were first and foremost authoritarian thugs who manipulated ideology to suit their needs. But they serve as ongoing reminders that the linear political spectrum is inherently flawed.

Economics does a marginally better job of distinguishing left-wing and right-wing thinking – although I don't think the divide need be as big as we've traditionally made it.

Founding fathers

Let's start by putting two of the founding fathers of economics at either end of the spectrum: Karl Marx on the left and Adam Smith to the right. A Scot, writing in the late eighteenth century, Smith was the Enlightenment-era optimist fascinated by the power of commerce to drive progress. His peers were philosophers like David Hume, Immanuel Kant, John Locke and Voltaire. To be fair to Smith, the terms left and right hadn't even been coined for political alignment at the time. They originate from the seating arrangements in the post-revolutionary French Parliament.

Given Smith's enthusiasm for the betterment of the masses, a case can be made that he was originally more of a liberal progressive – certainly by the low standards of the day. He is regarded as the first modern economist. While other philosophers throughout history contemplated money and its place in social organisation, Smith made it its own discipline. He laid out and defined notions like supply and demand, division of labour and international trade.

But his most radical idea – in a world that was still highly religious and puritanical – was that all this stuff was good. He didn't quite go as far as to declare 'greed is good', like the anti-hero Gordon Gekko in the 1987 film *Wall Street*. But he argued the motivation to acquire wealth was a powerful and valuable force. He said that trade on a free market was mutually beneficial to all involved.

'It is not from the benevolence of the butcher, the brewer, or the baker that we expect our dinner, but from their regard for their own interest,' Smith wrote in his 1776 epic *An Inquiry into the Nature and Causes of the Wealth of Nations*. The book is considered the founding text of classical economics. It also runs to about 1000 pages, and if you are really keen to read more Smith I'd recommend the late American satirist P.J. O'Rourke's hilarious summary *On the Wealth of Nations* (2007).

In Smith's ideal economy a financial transaction didn't need a winner and a loser. If the market were free, then the price would be fair, and we would all win. It's not hard to see why these days he remains beloved by right-wing think tanks the world over.

Smith's *Wealth of Nations* attracted plenty of critics from the outset. But it would be almost a century before another philosopher with a similar passion for economics captured the popular imagination with his own polarising rebuttal of classical economics.

Karl Marx is famously the architect of socialism and communism, although the bulk of his work was backward-looking, an analysis of human economic history. He was the original critic of capitalism. A German expat living in London from 1849, he was a pessimist writing in the immediate wake of the Industrial Revolution, a time of radical technological change and scientific advance. He looked at all the inequality and poverty he saw in nineteenth-century Europe and concluded that capitalism was not good.

While Smith and Marx viewed money and wealth through very different lenses, they also had plenty in common – and Marx was certainly influenced by Smith, whose work had become widely celebrated. Both were philosophers who recognised that economics was about the organised allocation of resources. It was the algorithm that built civilisation and lifted us above all other species. Both accepted that money was fundamental to society and that only by putting an agreed price on things could we bargain and trade. As we touched on in the last chapter, you can't build a civilisation until you agree on the value of things.

Keynes vs Friedman — the battle we're still fighting

Smith and Marx give us the foundations of political thinking about economics, but it is a divide between two twentieth-century economic thinkers that holds sway over the modern political landscape.

The difference of opinion between John Maynard Keynes and Milton Friedman goes to the heart of economic debate over the past century. If you follow economics even half-heartedly, it won't be long before you hear policies described as Keynesian or monetarist. So, who were these guys and what do those terms mean?

An Oxford-educated Englishman, Keynes was hugely influential in managing Western economies through World War Two and the years of reconstruction and recovery through the 1950s and 1960s. He sought a way to moderate the capitalist excesses that had led to the Great Depression of the 1930s, yet without the violent revolutions that communism had unleashed in places like the Soviet Union. At the most basic level, he believed in central control of the demand side of the economy using government spending and taxation (what we call fiscal policies).

Keynes argued that cash spent by governments would always work its way back through an economy, so it wasn't wasted — and of course, it could be invested in large-scale projects that were hard to organise privately and which would enhance the productive efficiency of an economy. Bridges, roads and railways, which allow the faster transport of goods, and big power plants that reduce energy costs: these are all examples of infrastructure projects governments can build that should enhance the overall performance of the economy.

In an era when unfettered capitalism was blamed for the damage wrought by the Wall Street Crash in 1929, the Depression and subsequent global conflict, Keynes' policies were embraced enthusiastically. During World War Two, his ideas around central government command and control of the economies was critical to the eventual military success of the Allied forces. In the wake of the war, massive works of reconstruction were needed, and across the Western world voters returned governments that ran policies of large-scale intervention and control of economies.

Keynesian policies continued to dominate political thinking in the West through to the 1970s. But during that era, another key economic figure was quietly hatching some other ideas that would sweep the world.

US economist Milton Friedman was born in Brooklyn in 1912 to working-class immigrant parents. He was suspicious of state control. Friedman and his followers — sometimes called Friedmanites, but more broadly described as monetarists — saw inflation and instability in the value of money as the biggest issue in an economy.

Freidman favoured control of the supply side of an economy, so sometimes you'll also hear his ideas described as supply-side economics. In other words, he argued that if central banks could keep a tight control on the money supply, ensuring price stability, then we'd have a level playing field and commerce could lead the way.

'Inflation is always and everywhere a monetary phenomenon,' he famously wrote. It is a powerful mantra and one that is still key to how we run our modern economies, with central banks using their tools around pricing money to control its supply and ensure price stability. By raising or lowering interest rates, the supply and flow of money can be constricted or expanded to balance out the economic ups and downs that events may cause.

Typically, left-leaning political parties are more embracing of Keynesian policy. Right-leaning parties are harder-line monetarists. During the 1960s, Friedman was an outspoken critic of the dominant Keynesian economic policies. But he got little traction until the oil shocks of the 1970s sent inflationary waves throughout the world. Prices started to spiral, economic growth faltered, and Keynesian policies didn't seem to have an answer. Monetarist policies were embraced by a new generation of political leaders like Ronald Reagan and Margaret Thatcher.

The debate between Keynesian and monetarist policies is a pendulum that continues to swing back and forth with big events. The monetarists, who had the upper hand through the 1980s and 1990s, were dealt another blow with the Global Financial Crisis, which prompted a return to Keynesian ideas of using fiscal policy to stimulate the economy. In response to huge escalation in wealth inequality, politicians on the left have become more vocal about direct policy intervention in economies with calls for higher progressive taxes.

After the GFC, central bankers were prepared to risk inflationary side effects to pump money into the economy with artificially low interest rates and even large-scale money printing. The global economy was still unwinding those GFC policies when the Covid-19 pandemic hit, requiring another round of Keynesian-style fiscal stimulus and interventionist policies from central banks.

But the emergence of inflation in the wake of the pandemic has served as a reminder that monetarist policies are still a vital part of the economic equation.

Ugly politics

History offers plenty of examples of horrible outcomes when trust in the economic system collapses. In Germany between the wars, the Nazi Party thrived in an economy where financial stability had broken down. In fact, that era was chaotic all around the world as the Wall Street Crash of 1929 flowed into the Great Depression. Unfettered capitalism had spiralled out of control and then collapsed, taking trust in the financial and political establishments with it.

We still see that kind of social breakdown today when poverty in developing nations creates political instability, which then generates more poverty. Booms and busts, inflation, deflation, economic contraction, unemployment and then social unrest — there's no shortage of ways an economy can go wrong in the modern world.

Smith saw capitalism as a force for wealth creation which could benefit all society if it was embraced freely and openly; Marx saw it as a system built by those in power to maintain their position. Greed, envy, theft, fraud, poverty, war: money is a constant driving force (although religious belief must also take a bow). The allocation of resources is the conflict that drives human history, said Marx.

Marx didn't see Smith's laws of supply and demand or division of labour as absolute and natural, but as a rest stop on the path of cultural evolution. He was so attuned to the inequity and social injustice in his world that he had to see it as a failing model. Humans had evolved from hunter–gatherers to slavers and feudal farmers and then to industrial capitalists. Surely, thought Marx, society will keep evolving and improving. He envisioned a highly efficient, rational world where private property and excessive wealth were banished in favour of collective ownership, with production organised cooperatively.

Perhaps the distant future still holds the prospect of such a utopian social structure. But efforts by followers of Marx to build post-capitalist societies in the twentieth century haven't provided any compelling evidence yet. In fact, his ideas inspired some of the worst social and economic failures in history. Tragically there have been revolutions, wars and even genocides committed by those professing to be followers of Karl Marx. Former New Zealand politician Richard Prebble, who shifted his allegiance from the left wing to the right, once argued that 'when the government takes everything, people stop working. The result is famine. Thirty million Chinese starved to death in the Great Leap Forward.'

Prebble was right (if perhaps a little hyperbolic in using his example to condemn the moderate centre-left Labour government of Jacinda Ardern), Mao Zedong's Great Leap Forward of the late 1950s to early 1960s may represent the most extreme failing of a centralised command-and-control model (although others like the Khmer Rouge in Cambodia might give him a run for his money).

While the Chinese Communist Party certainly controlled everything, it was less about a demotivated workforce and more about the bad decisions by government. Allegedly bourgeois agricultural practices were dropped and, as a result, farm output dropped too. Mao's determination that China should lead the world in iron ore production also saw much effort shifted away from crucial agricultural efforts. The strict authoritarian regime made local politicians fearful of reporting accurate harvest records, and central government carried on in the false belief that there were surpluses when, in reality, the rural population was starving. Whatever the final mix of causes, it was an unmitigated disaster.

But if we're going to visit the extremes of political failure, it only seems fair to balance our argument by considering the equally nightmarish scenario of a world devoid of government and regulation. I'd describe that as the 'stateless warlord' model. Somalia in the 1990s is just one grim example.

If you want to live in a truly libertarian society, without any bureaucratic bother, good luck to you. Just make sure you have a sturdy machine-gun-mounted jeep and enough food to feed your gang of teenage mercenaries, in case they turn on you.

Both examples are absurd in the New Zealand context. I think we should be wary of extrapolating the excesses of communism and hard-line socialism to more moderate forms of government. Funnily enough, a lot of us quite like a central government based on a few high-minded human ideals. Without it, life would be 'nasty, brutish and short', as the seventeenth-century philosopher Thomas Hobbes put it.

In New Zealand, we're blessed with a broad social consensus around the role of the state in things like health, education, industry and finance. There are no major political parties advocating the dismantling of public healthcare or education. Nor are there any advocating for the nationalisation of private industry.

Unsurprisingly, enthusiasm for hard-line Marxism and communism has dwindled around the world in the twenty-first century. The private sector has proved itself better at designing and building things than the public sector. (As I've hinted earlier, I've always argued that the inability to design a decent pair of jeans was one of the underlying reasons why the Soviet Union failed. The Soviets couldn't compete with America on making cool stuff, and they lost the support of their young people.) The most successful remaining communist regimes, such as China and Vietnam, are effectively running a mixed model, with plenty of capitalism going on despite the centrally controlled oversight.

But since the GFC, belief in the power of free markets to deliver positive outcomes has also faded. There is a loose consensus on the need to balance freedom and regulation, albeit with intense arguments still raging about how we strike that balance. That is heartening — or it would be if the economic debate weren't being swamped by culture wars.

So, who was right?

The great thing about economics is that everyone can have an opinion. There are plenty of facts. But it's a science that is never quite settled. Unlike hard sciences, which can run countless lab-controlled experiments, economics is mostly theory. We only get to observe economic experiments once, in real time, as our choices play out. We never get to see the counterfactual — the alternative outcomes that might have been possible with small tweaks or different policy approaches.

In my mind Smith and Marx are the yin and yang of economic thinking. Without one, the other becomes untethered and unbalanced. Both men need to be viewed in historical context, and I'd be suspicious of anyone who claimed to be a follower of one or the other. Both offered crucial insights into the economic behaviour of humans, but the ideas of neither should be treated as some sort of absolute model for society.

Their ideas remain at the heart of political debate in economics — essentially a difference of opinion about the merits of centralised control and regulation versus individual action and regulatory freedom. The tension between the two outlooks remains strong in modern life because both outlooks still hold moral weight. How we find the right balance and mix still leaves the world's political pundits with plenty to argue about.

Chapter 4

Good times, bad times

I would rather have this country free from
want and squalor and unemployed than
the home of multi-millionaires.
— NZ Premier Richard 'King Dick' Seddon, 1905

....

My generation grew up and came of age through one of the most interesting periods for politics and economics in New Zealand's history. I would say that, of course, and another generation might make the same case for their era. Certainly, the kids who grew up in the time of Trump and Covid-19 will have stories to tell. But compared with the relative stability of the 1960s — where Keith Holyoake's National Party ruled for four successive terms — or the Helen Clark and John Key era of the early 2000s, the 1970s to the early 1990s were a wild rollercoaster ride in which New Zealand underwent a rapid period of economic change.

It's an era that still casts a shadow on the modern economic landscape, so it's one that I will keep coming back to when we look at more specific economic issues in later chapters. If nothing else, the big shift in thinking through that era provides an excellent case study of the two main ways of looking at an economy. It's also the era that shaped my life and my thinking so, I'll admit it, I'm biased.

So I'm going to dive deep into the 1970s and the economic trauma that inspired 15 years of reform through the 1980s–90s. I'm also going to look at the postwar economic booms and busts that shaped the modern economy. And we can't ignore the biggest bust of all: the Great

Depression. First, though, let's go even further back and take a quick detour through the colonial era.

New Zealand's early colonial economy was based on sealing and whaling, timber and gold. Economist Brian Easton canvasses the era in his 2009 paper 'It's The Same This Time? Cycles and Depressions in New Zealand History'.[1] Many of the initial economic ups and downs were related to supply issues, delays and disruptions in acquiring resources from Britain. Other times they simply related to the depletion of resources — like the demise of the kauri gum trade as the great forests were felled and the gum fields exhausted. Or the boom and bust of the great Otago gold rush.

Things started to stabilise in the 1860s as the rise of sheep farming and wool exports to the UK delivered a steady stream of export revenue. Off the sheep's back, popular Premier Julius Vogel (no relation to the delicious bread) and his government borrowed and invested heavily to build roads and railways. The country boomed through the 1870s.

But an economic shock put Britain and many other parts of Europe into a serious downturn in the 1880s, referred to as the Long Depression. In 1878, the City of Glasgow Bank went bust, triggering a financial crisis and credit crunch in the UK. This affected New Zealand in two ways, writes Easton.

'First, the bank had made speculative investments in Australia and New Zealand, in the hope of recouping banking losses. Second, and following three further bank collapses in December, there was a tightening in the London money market.' Easton continues: 'New Zealand had spent the previous decade relying on borrowing in London to support the Vogel boom. The tap was turned off and there was a credit contraction.'

Compounding things, the global downturn saw wool prices fall. So, we were earning less and couldn't afford to borrow more. Also, in what seems

1   Brian Easton, 'It's the Same This Time? Cycles and Depressions in New Zealand History', *Policy Quarterly*, vol. 5, no. 1 (2009), DOI: 10.26686.pq.v5i1.4286.

like a depressingly familiar story some 150 years later, Easton notes that 'there had been land speculation in the 1870s, including irresponsible lending by banks (as the City of Glasgow Bank story suggests) but also fuelled by the government borrowing of the Vogel era'. A debt-fuelled spend-up created a property bubble, which was followed by a financial meltdown and a tough period of austerity.

If it all sounds a bit familiar, it is, because New Zealand has repeated this cycle several times in its history. In a way, this was the first of the dreaded 'external shocks' that finance ministers still worry about and prepare for to this day. As a small trading nation, New Zealand is at the mercy of the global economy in a way that countries with larger populations (and larger domestic economies) aren't.

The 1880s must have been a long, tough decade, with grand plans for nation-building suddenly on hold; but there was one ray of economic hope in the era. New Zealand's first successful shipment of frozen meat left for Britain in 1882. A British-based entrepreneur, William Soltau Davidson, whose combined landholdings here and in the UK exceeded a million hectares, turned what had previously been an experimental concept into a commercially viable operation that effectively pioneered long-distance meat exports.

When the UK bounced back in the 1890s, our meat and wool exports boomed. The following decades were to be no barrel of laughs, tragically, as Europe went to war and we followed, with the deadly Spanish flu coming straight after. Economically, however, New Zealand came through well due to a guaranteed supply and pricing agreement with the UK. We were ready to roar into the 1920s and the twentieth century.

RECESSION

Any discussion about economic cycles ought to involve a balanced look at the good times and the bad.

Most modern developed economies spend more time in growth than in recession. If they didn't, we might not be so inclined to tolerate capitalism, with all of its excesses and inequities. But let's face it, recessions are the headline-grabbers. Everyone knows that recession is the real bogeyman of economics, the grim reaper of boom times, the destroyer of wealth. Recession is a super-villain, the economic catastrophe we're all taught to fear.

What we want with an economy is a boring platform of stable moderate growth presenting plenty of opportunities for people to better themselves. That doesn't make for a great story, though. People don't write many novels or love songs about life tracking along in a moderately nice fashion. We are obsessed with bad times — perhaps because they help us appreciate and make sense of the good times.

So, what exactly is a recession? Most people who follow economics would probably describe it as two successive quarters in which an economy contracts, displaying what economists often annoyingly describe as 'negative growth'. It's a time when it feels like things are generally getting worse, not better. People worry about their jobs and save, instead of spend; so there is less money in circulation, and it is moving through the economy at a slower rate.

Two consecutive quarters of recession is the closest thing we have to a technical definition of recession, but it has never been fully accepted by economists as an official definition. That's because it's completely arbitrary. For starters, it's worth pointing out that two quarters (i.e. two periods of three months) is what normal people call six months! Or half a year. Whatever: economists and accountants like to break the year into quarters.

I guess two of them seems like a period that is long enough to consider significant if you have spent all of it down in the dumps. (It's a good thing we don't let economists define mental depression: 'Sorry, but you weren't quite sad enough in the March quarter; no Prozac for you!')

Recessions can be short and sharp, they can be long and shallow. Even that specific choice of two successive quarters distorts how we define what might more colloquially be called an economic downturn.

Imagine a year where the first three months see very low, slow growth; in the second three months there is a deep contraction, followed by another flat quarter with a very small uptick in growth, and then the final quarter sees another deep contraction. That's a rough year in anyone's book. Clearly the economy has gone backwards — but it doesn't meet the technical definition of recession.

The government gets to trumpet the news that the economy has avoided recession. The media are cursing that they didn't get to run headlines containing the dreaded r— word. The rest of us ordinary punters would still be left worrying about cost-cutting at work and redundancy, or lack of cashflow if we were in business ourselves. But perhaps we'd feel buoyed by the headlines. Perhaps that would convince us to go and spend. And perhaps that would actually boost the economy.

Economies are the sum of our collective behaviour, and if we all start to believe a recession is coming, then there is a risk that we'll collectively adjust our behaviour. That adjustment can in itself be recessionary. If we spend too much time worrying about recessions, they can become self-fulfilling prophecies. So, of course, like a lot of economics, how and when we start talking about recession is highly political.

That's one reason why, in the US, a recession has to be declared formally by a committee — the National Bureau of Economic Research. The committee that does the assessing is guided by the two-quarter technical definition, but it reserves the right to apply qualitative judgements. It looks at what are sometimes called classical measures, such as unemployment and the general vibe of the economy.

In New Zealand we don't muck around with committees. Good luck telling anyone we're not in recession if that second-quarter GDP number dips below zero.

After the grim years of the Great War and flu pandemic, New Zealand was doing okay. But we'd started running some conservative economic policies through the 1920s and early 1930s. Whatever legacy we had as a progressive liberal country — such as being the first democracy to give women the vote — had fallen away. We were a cautious bunch, and a conservative party was firmly in charge of the country. The Reform Party, under Prime Minister William Massey, took control of government in 1911. Reform stayed in power until 1935 — albeit in a coalition with the United Party from 1928 (which would eventually combine to become the National Party).

It must have seemed a very stable period for many Kiwis as they settled into postwar life and set about building their quarter-acre paradises. New Zealanders wouldn't notice it for months afterwards, but the world changed in October 1929 when Wall Street crashed.

What's so great about a depression?

If the concept of recession is only loosely defined, there are no guidelines at all for what constitutes a depression. There are certainly no rules about what makes one 'great'. There's no set period an economy must contract for, nor any specific percentage by which GDP needs to fall. But depressions are serious, world-shaking events. There have only really been two in modern history: the Long Depression of the 1880s and the Great Depression from 1929 to 1939.

Of course, the Great Depression looms much larger in our collective consciousness. Its reputation isn't just down to the money and jobs that were lost or the economic hardship of the era. The Great Depression's place in history is tied to the social and political revolutions that it sparked. In Europe that ended with the rise of fascism and, ultimately, war.

But there was also a more positive revolution. In the US, UK and New Zealand the upheaval led to the rise of the welfare state, the labour movement and those big interventionist government policies championed by John Maynard Keynes.

So, what actually happened?

In the US the 1920s had roared. A speculative investment bubble grew rapidly on capital markets as people rode the wealth, creating a wave of automation and industrialisation that rose to giddy heights. Wall Street's Dow Jones Industrial Average increased sixfold from August 1921 to September 1929. (The Dow is an index of 30 major companies listed on US stock exchanges, and serves as a pretty good barometer of the state of equity markets.)

After prices peaked, US economist Irving Fisher made the infamous and ill-fated proclamation, 'Stock prices have reached what looks like a permanently high plateau.' This was the time of those stock-tipping shoeshine boys. It seemed everyone was in on it.

Then, on Black Monday, 28 October 1929, the Dow plunged nearly 13 per cent. The next day, Black Tuesday, the market dropped nearly 12 per cent. I think there was a Black Thursday in there somewhere, too, but you get the picture.

This is the market meltdown that defines them all. It is the one that gave us the sad, cartoonish trope of stockbrokers throwing themselves out of skyrise windows. For the record, while the suicide reports circulated widely at the time, researchers now believe they were the stuff of urban legend.

The financial and economic damage was very real, though. There's no question that fortunes were lost and lives were ruined. By mid-November 1929, the market had lost almost half of its value. By the middle of 1932, the Dow was 89 per cent below its peak. It didn't recover to its pre-crash high until November 1954.

New Zealand was a long way from the action, of course; the market meltdown made only a brief news item in the *Herald* several days after the event. But the fallout spread, causing a big slump in global trade as countries tried to protect themselves with tariffs. That soon hit Great Britain. And once our major trading partner began suffering, New Zealand couldn't avoid the Great Depression.

Unfortunately, after many years in power the government in New Zealand was too entrenched and too conservative to make the kind of bold policy moves needed. As *Te Ara* (the Encyclopedia of New Zealand) puts it, 'the depression was aggravated by New Zealand's extreme unpreparedness to meet it'. We had limited social welfare and no unemployment benefit in place. As unemployment spiked and tax revenue fell, the coalition government attempted to balance the books by cutting spending — a policy we now sometimes call fiscal austerity.

While it can seem like a good idea to cut costs when times get tough, history suggests that it can often make things worse. When it comes to the day-to-day experience of economics, people find meaning in factors like job security, the cost of living, and a sense of progress towards being wealthier as opposed to feeling poorer. To a large extent these things rely on the public retaining confidence in the immediate future, which is why the threat of recession can cause real fear and panic. It can cause investors to shut up shop, lenders to become very conservative, deals to fall over. People become risk-averse and stop investing in the more productive industries, such as technology, that will improve the economy. They get nervous and start hoarding wealth, which takes cash out of the economy.

Nowadays, central banks push back against that kind of economic decline by cutting interest rates to encourage more lending and more spending. In other words, we lower the cost of borrowing. Policymakers want to keep money circulating and being used to do stuff and buy stuff. In extreme cases, as with the GFC and the pandemic, central banks literally create more money with tools like quantitative easing (see page 92).

When confidence disappears from an economy it creates a kind of negative spiral. To cut costs, businesses halt wage rises and cut back on hiring new staff. When cash is tight, they reduce spending on everything from stationery to travel. They're also reluctant to take risk and spend money on investing in future growth, through channels such as advertising and new product development. That means less money flowing to contracts and other businesses that provide services. Eventually it means laying off staff.

Mass unemployment and business failure did terrible damage during the Great Depression. It shook public faith in government institutions, which played a big part in sending the world back to war.

When things get as bad as they did in the 1930s, counting quarters of negative GDP growth all starts to seem a bit meaningless. In 2008, when the world was on the brink of a 1929-style financial market collapse, economic commentators hedged their bets and called the post-GFC downturn the Great Recession. That was a way of saying things were worse than a usual recession, but not as bad as the 1930s.

I remember talking about the Great Depression with my grandfather Colin, sometime around 2008. I was in the thick of covering the GFC and fearful that we hadn't yet seen the worst of it. I suspect that handling screeds of alarming news-wire stories about the crisis all day wasn't helping my mind-set.

I suggested to my grandfather that this could be spiralling into something like the Great Depression. Colin, who was born in 1913, came of age during the Great Depression. He was an affable man and a very kind grandparent. If he ever got angry, I never saw it. But he laughed at me that time. I don't think he meant to; he just couldn't help it.

He went on to share some Depression-era memories — things like seeing men in town queuing up for buses to take them out onto the Canterbury Plains to plant pines on government work schemes. I went on to get a grip.

It's not hard to see how my comparing the Depression with a modern downturn in this consumer-driven world of mobile phones and designer sneakers didn't stack up for him. In the GFC years, our unemployment rate peaked below seven per cent (although it went as high as 17 per cent for young people). According to the Reserve Bank, unemployment topped 30 per cent in New Zealand during the Great Depression.

There were riots and civil unrest, and support for the fledgling Labour Party swelled. Under the charismatic leadership of a slight, bespectacled Australian, Michael Joseph Savage, the party of the workers (and the unemployed) swept to a landslide victory in 1935.

Labour remained in power until 1949, winning four terms, which gave the government scope to transform the country into one of the world's most progressive welfare states. The Bank of New Zealand was nationalised, as were coalmines, domestic air services, broadcasting and transport. Drawing on Keynesian economics, Labour stimulated New Zealand's depressed economy by lifting wage rates, launching a programme of public works (including the large-scale building of state housing), and expanding healthcare and other benefits through the Social Security Act of 1938.

To quote *Te Ara* (again), these policies set the framework for political debate in New Zealand for the next 40 years: 'Neither Labour's welfare state nor its mixed economy was seriously challenged until the 1980s.' Which is, of course, about where my generation joins the story.

Chapter 5

Muldoon's shadow

They won't put up a statue to me. No, no, no.
Nobody's got that sense of humour.
— Sir Robert Muldoon

....

My childhood was a middle-class one, with primary school teacher parents and a sense that I lived a very normal, modern suburban life. We didn't have much spare money, but we did all the things Kiwi families did in those days: camping, tramping, busing to town to watch the latest movies. International travel — Disneyland being the dream — was out of reach, but so it was to most of the families we grew up around. So we felt very normal.

My father's politics were rooted in the working-class Labour values that stretched back to faith in the party's beloved first prime minister, Michael Joseph Savage. Dad's political outlook was honed by his love of US blue-collar intellectualism, popularised by the beat generation and folk singers, just as he was coming of age in the 1950s and early 1960s. Whether it was heated debate at the dinner table or just Dad shouting at the television news, we were never in any doubt that politics was a powerful and meaningful force in the world.

More often than not, the target of Dad's rage was Robert Muldoon. The larger-than-life prime minister, who came to power in the campaign of 1975, was the first leader of the colour-television age in New Zealand and his presence dominated our screens. They were great days for political satire. We lapped up the irreverent impersonations of comedians like

David McPhail and the stark caricatures of cartoonist Peter Bromhead. The comic genius of John Clarke, whom we knew for his character Fred Dagg, was forged in the fires of Robert Muldoon's New Zealand. There were 'piggy' Muldoon money boxes, there were jokes and songs.

There's a reason the satire and comedy of the 1970s was so obsessed with mocking rules and bureaucracy. It ruled people's lives. New Zealand was a place where you needed a sticker on your car to tell you which days you could drive. It was a time when Parliament could freeze wages and prices.

Muldoon was a National Party prime minister, conservative and theoretically right-wing. His 1975 campaign involved an infamous cartoon TV ad which warned of a left-wing government takeover and ended with a row of dancing Cossacks — implying that Labour's state-run pension scheme would lead us to communism. But Muldoon was also a veteran of World War Two and a product of the postwar reconstruction where the centralised command-and-control economics of John Maynard Keynes had flourished. He championed a 'think big' policy of large-scale state investment in ambitious industrial projects, such as the Bluff aluminium smelter and Marsden Point oil refinery.

He was a defender of state subsidies and tariffs to protect local businesses, and of restrictions on foreign imports. Retailers needed licences to bring in the latest electronic gadgets like digital watches or high-end stereo equipment. Even international records had an import duty on them, leading to a boom in locally produced albums of dubious artistic merit.

The opportunity for the tariffs to bolster the more creative end of the local industry was squandered, though, by a decision to retain a 40 per cent sales tax on local records, making only the most commercial TV talent show variety artists particularly viable.

The only upside of the sales tax debate was that it inspired the excellent Kiwi punk rock single 'Culture' by the Knobz. New Zealand made its own TVs and appliances, shoes, and own-brand jeans and sportswear. Some of that sounds quite nice now in a globalised world where we are often overwhelmed with cheap disposable imports. But the problem was that much of our home-made stuff wasn't as good — and we knew it. We could no longer keep up with the pace of technological change.

As children in the 1970s, even authentic Lego was a rare treat. We relied on Aussie relatives bringing it in through duty-free shops. Meanwhile, we had to struggle with the unwieldy and chunky local version — Torro. We would longingly stare at the adverts in US comics for Hubba Bubba and Twinkies and all manner of unobtainable action figurines.

It's possible my generation felt the isolation more acutely because global media was rubbing it in our face in a way it didn't for older Kiwis. *Star Wars*, for instance, landed in US cinemas in May 1977, and *Star Wars* mania swept the world. But the movie didn't reach New Zealand until the December holidays six months later.

By the early 1980s, as a new wave of US consumerism swept the world, New Zealand was starting to feel like a backwater. That might have been all right if we were still living in the golden economic era of the 1960s. But we weren't.

So, before we finish off this historic journey of booms and busts, we should probably consider the good times.

Okay, boomer

As I've noted earlier, New Zealand has a long history of cycling in and out of recession — and as a journalist looking for drama and conflict, I tend to focus on those bits. But we do occasionally remember the good times. The postwar era through to the 1970s often seems romanticised and overly mythologised by the baby-boom generation, but it really was one of the biggest economic booms this country has ever seen.

The history of booms and busts in this country — until the GFC, at least — has been comprehensively examined by Reserve Bank economists John McDermott and Viv Hall. In their 2014 work 'Recessions and Recoveries in New Zealand's Post-Second World War Business Cycles', they make the point that the technical definition of recession is often insufficient to capture the true state of the economy.[2]

Using what they describe as 'the easy-to-follow, frequently used practice of calling a recession immediately after two successive quarters of negative real GDP growth have been published', Hall and McDermott conclude that since the Second World War, New Zealand has been through 11 completed peak-to-peak cycles and 12 contractionary phases, up to and including the post-GFC recession. This compares with the eight classical cycles and nine contractionary phases defined using a broader more qualitative 'classical' methodology. By either measure it's fair to say that the baby boomers' fond memories of the 1950s and 1960s are more than just nostalgia.

Hill and McDermott looked at the whole scope of postwar economic cycles in New Zealand and they counted the quarters. From 1952, the economy grew for 58 quarters in a row, and by 86.7 per cent, until a short, sharp crash in the wool market — which then accounted for 31 per cent of our exports — ended the long boom run in 1967. That was not just a long boom, it was also a steep one. Economic growth was rapid, so people could really feel times getting better. By comparison, the so-called rock star economy years of the John Key government — from the end of the 2009 recession to 2017 — represented 34 quarters of consecutive growth. But overall the economy grew just 26 per cent, representing much slower growth relative to the golden era boom.

If we take the broader view of recession, the economy at the time pretty much took the wool price crash and recession of 1967 in its stride. It certainly doesn't feature in our popular history the way other slumps do. It helped that unemployment was very low, and the recession so short that the social impact was limited.

Anyway, if you look through the short recession of 1967, you can make the case that the golden era of benign economic growth lasted all the way

---

2   Viv B. Hall and C. John McDermott, 'Recessions and Recoveries in New Zealand's Post-Second World War Business Cycles', Reserve Bank of New Zealand Te Pūtea Matua, July 2014, www.rbnz. govt.nz/-/media/project/sites/rbnz/files/publications/discussion-papers/2014/dp14-02.pdf.

from 1952 to the oil shock in 1976 (which would usher in a deeper, more structurally damaging recession). The 1950s, 1960s and early 1970s left New Zealand near the top of all the OECD charts for per capita wealth and incomes.

Of course, the strength of the economy through that era needs to be viewed in the context of the miserable decades that preceded it. If my parents' generation got lucky, their parents sure didn't, what with the Great Depression, the war, and then the economic hardship in its immediate aftermath. New Zealand also experienced recession in 1946 and 1947. That's much as we have found in the years following the Covid-19 pandemic. Life doesn't just pick up where it left off after years of social and economic trauma. It takes a while to get back on track.

The UK, our primary export market, was still an economic mess in the late 1940s, with bombed-out buildings, and ration books limiting consumer spending. It took years for normal global trade to resume. But America, which escaped the direct infrastructure damage of the war, was booming and investing in Europe with the Marshall Plan.

The US, seeking to sell the world on capitalism and head off communism, was actively fostering an open environment for the world to expand. It was creating new markets for its goods. Even Germany and Japan thrived. And when the switch flipped, New Zealand, with its infrastructure and farming systems also largely untroubled by the war, was ready and waiting to make the most of the new environment, with exports of meat, dairy and wool.

It was into that era of economic expansion, with both private productivity surging and big Keynesian government investing back into the economy, that the baby boomers were born. By the 1960s, there was a youthquake under way overseas. Rock'n'roll, television, civil rights, blue jeans, women's lib, peace and love . . . the boomers knew they had it good (although they seemed to get pretty sick of being told that by their elders). And all that pop culture and modern consumerism eventually even made it to New Zealand. We embraced the movies, the TV and the music, even though we were still a closed economy.

End of the golden weather

At the start of the 1970s, it must have felt like New Zealand was on a roll. The economy was still strong and, after more than a decade of conservative government, Labour swept back into power in November 1972 with a burly, populist prime minister, Norman Kirk. Big Norm was a liberal. He opposed the Vietnam War, supported calls to stop playing rugby against South Africa and publicly opposed French nuclear testing in the Pacific.

In my idealised narrative imagining of the era, that summer of 1972/73 must have been dreamy for young Kiwis. Our Woodstock was the Great Ngaruawahia Music Festival, held just north of Hamilton in January 1973 — headlined by Black Sabbath but stacked with legendary local performers like Split Enz, Blerta and Dragon. Tens of thousands of optimistic long-haired young New Zealanders gathered in a paddock, stripped off, painted their faces and danced in the sun, swigging brown bottles of crate beer and dreaming of the good days ahead.

Sadly, though, the beginning of the end of the golden weather was closer than they could have imagined. Britain formally became a full member of the European Economic Community on 1 January 1973.

Suddenly, tough European tariffs were imposed on sales of our meat, wool, butter and cheese. In October that year, the world experienced the first oil price shock as the Arab nations got organised and formed OPEC (Organization of the Petroleum Exporting Countries). Our export earnings plunged, and our import costs spiked. Government borrowing and spending filled the shortfall. Labour had delivered a record budget surplus after its first year in office, but by 1974 inflation was building.

Then in 1974, Kirk died suddenly, dealing a blow to the liberal causes he championed. His finance minister, Bill Rowling, was a smart, likeable man, but when he became the Labour leader he was no match for the political force that was Rob Muldoon. With his hard-nosed conservative values and warnings of communism, Muldoon swept National into power in 1975. He didn't radically change the way the economy was run. In fact, as noted earlier, he doubled down on attempts to shield New Zealand from the fallout of the global economic storm. He kept borrowing and imposed tariffs to protect local businesses. It didn't halt the economic slide, and by 1976 we were officially in recession. It was a long one — seven quarters of contraction.

After that, effectively for the bulk of my childhood and young adult years, New Zealand was in and out of recession so often that the spectre of economic downturn was always present. According to Hall and McDermott, New Zealand had recessions again in 1982 and 1983, again through 1987–88, a brief expansion, and then another recession in 1991. But to all intents and purposes it felt like just one long downturn. The long boom was over, leaving my generation — angry, cynical Generation X — feeling forever jaded about our economic lot.

In his final term in power, Muldoon really began to lose control of the economy. With both wages and prices spiralling out of control, he introduced policies that now seem almost authoritarian. He attempted to end inflation by decree, bringing in a nationwide price and wage freeze in 1982. He tried to curb petrol consumption with his 'carless days' policy, forcing drivers to choose a day on which they were forbidden to drive. It was a hopelessly ill-conceived policy which forced many Kiwi families — including ours — to buy a second car just to get through their weekly routines.

Muldoon had unwittingly headed off on a path of Big Government, running a command-and-control economy that was veering oddly close to socialism. But his backing of the NZ Rugby Union and support for a tour by the apartheid-era South African rugby team put him squarely back in the conservative camp. In fact, it was probably what kept him in power.

The cultural war Muldoon fought over the 1981 Springbok tour is one of the most well-traversed social conflicts in New Zealand's modern history. It sowed intense social division, and saw riots and pitched battles in the streets around the tour matches.

The violence and unrest leading up to and during the tour were underpinned by a strong moral argument. Kiwis were standing up to a racist regime in South Africa, but also venting their frustration about the oppressive dominance of a culture in which rugby was sacrosanct. The social split fell in Muldoon's favour, though; it distracted from the faltering economy and likely won him the election in 1981, albeit by the narrowest of margins.

The next three years of increasingly erratic economic leadership almost proved disastrous for New Zealand. 'There is No Depression in New Zealand' sang the post-punk Kiwi band Blam Blam Blam sarcastically in 1981. Actually, there wasn't a depression — not quite. There sure was a recession, though, and unemployment was rising fast. Statistically, it wasn't as grim for New Zealand as it would be in the late 1980s and early 1990s. But in the wake of the long economic boom of the 1950s–60s it felt pretty bad.

Our once world-leading standard of living was being propped up by government spending, the national debt was skyrocketing and — with inflation gripping the world — the borrowing costs were endangering our financial stability. New Zealand was slowly going bankrupt. The world didn't want our lamb or wool, and nobody was quite sure what was going to replace them as our major export earner. The dairy boom and Chinese consumer demand were decades away. Kiwifruit and wine were promising but tiny export industries.

In the days before Peter Jackson showed off our scenery to the world, the idea of having a major international tourist industry seemed laughable; who would want to come to a backwater like New Zealand? When the Rolling Stones toured, Mick Jagger allegedly called Invercargill the arsehole of the world. Perhaps it sparked a bit of faux outrage in the papers — but quietly a lot of Kiwis, especially the younger generation, were inclined to agree.

All the rules, regulation and red tape holding the economy together were also limiting opportunities for young people, and they began heading offshore in record numbers. Fears about a 'brain drain' of our brightest and most educated — primarily to Australia — were prompted by falling net migration rates from the early 1970s, which moved into a net loss territory from 1976.

Muldoon's response was glib and parochial, but popular. 'New Zealanders who leave for Australia raise the IQ of both countries,' he famously quipped. It was funny, but it wasn't true. Young people had had a gutsful of the malaise gripping the country. They were bored, angry and anxious for change.

Chapter 6

A brave
new world

Government is not the solution to our problem;
government is the problem.
— Ronald Reagan, Inaugural Address, 1981

....

In July 1984, after drunkenly calling a snap election, Muldoon was turfed out of power. A new and equally imposing figure, David Lange, led a new model of Labour government onto the political stage. But in some respects, the economic and cultural low point of the Muldoon era occurred after it was officially over.

The Queen Street riots loom like a symbolic book-end to the era of youthful optimism I romanticised earlier with the hippie love fest at Ngāruawāhia in 1973.

On Friday, 7 December 1984, thousands of young people went on a rampage down Auckland's Queen Street, smashing shop windows and overturning cars, after a free concert in Aotea Square, fronted by Dave Dobbyn with his band DD Smash, got seriously out of hand.

To modern sensibilities, the fact that Dobbyn — now a cultural pop icon of middle New Zealand — was at the centre of all the carnage seems a little comical. (For the record he was charged with, but later cleared of, inciting a riot.) But New Zealand — to use a colloquialism of the day — was as rough as guts in the 1970s and 1980s. There was clearly too much alcohol on hand in Aotea Square that day, and people had turned up to the event ready to get wasted.

It was, according to some historians, the worst example of civil unrest the country had seen since the 1932 riots by unemployed workers (also in Queen Street and at other centres around the country). Unlike those riots or the Springbok tour protests – which never saw that degree of vandalism and looting – it was a pointless and anarchistic incident, devoid of political merit. For that reason, I suspect it was at least partly rooted in the economic failures of the time.

The anarchistic mood in the nation wasn't helped by a financial meltdown a few months earlier as Muldoon was leaving office. Despite having conceded the election on 14 July, he refused to relinquish control of the tightly regulated Kiwi dollar until the formal hand-over of power was completed. There was a stand-off between the Reserve Bank governor, the new Labour government and Muldoon over the need to urgently devalue the dollar on Sunday, 15 July, before markets opened on the Monday.

Muldoon let slip, on a televised interview, that the Kiwi dollar would by devalued by Labour. That sparked fears which would see a dangerous run on the currency – a sell-off on global markets as traders tried to get ahead of the official move. Eventually, senior National leaders rebelled and talked Muldoon down. But to the international financial community, and the Kiwi public, this was economic chaos, and there was a very real sense that New Zealand was teetering on the edge of bankruptcy and banana republic status.

It's not hard to see why the young concertgoers in Aotea Square were feeling nihilistic by the end of the year. Radical change was coming, though.

The Fish and Chip Brigade

Weirdly, in New Zealand, the neoliberal, free-market theories of Milton Friedman that were sweeping back into fashion under Ronald Reagan's Republicans in the US and Margaret Thatcher's Conservative Party in the UK had been picked up by the young guns on the left. A new generation of liberals was following the 1960s social revolution of cultural and individual freedom down a surprisingly right-wing economic rabbit hole.

As a young teen in the 1980s, the new economics seemed entwined with a brave new world of sophistication and glamour — and freedom. The back-to-nature, communal ethos of the hippies was well and truly out of style, giving way to a brash materialism. It's a material world, Madonna declared. Let's make lots of money, whispered the Pet Shop Boys.

New Zealand was typically late to the eighties party, but under the new Labour government the country quickly made up for lost time. The dollar was floated, tariffs and subsidies were removed, taxes were lowered, the Reserve Bank was reformed and state assets were sold. Jeans were tapered. New Zealanders revelled in an open economy of cheap consumer imports. They also embraced the stock market with a naïve enthusiasm that would prove disastrous with the big crash of 1987.

ONE BLACK TUESDAY

While Wall Street's 22 per cent fall on Black Monday (19 October 1987) shocked the world, it was short-lived. Despite suffering the biggest single-day crash since 1929, the financial system did not seize up, the great Western economies did not stall.

For New Zealand, though, in the fervour of radical economic reform and deregulation, it was a financial disaster that some argue we never really recovered from. It was the day (Tuesday, 20 October here) on which we discovered that much of the new wealth that had been created with our new open economy was merely an illusion.

The cultural and social change in New Zealand through the mid-1980s coincided with one of the great global stock market runs, with the Dow Jones Industrial Average rising 282 per cent between 1982 and October 1987. The *Herald* business section's 1986 year in review described an unprecedented bullishness among local investors. It noted that 'white heat' in the market had some pessimists predicting a crash, but that the crash hadn't happened and 'the more optimistic were borrowing to invest more'.

'Through 1986, the share market became something of a national pastime,' says the article dated 2 January 1987. It added prophetically, 'Many average citizens flocked to the new off-course substitute TAB in the hope of catching profits before they were gone.' By February, the New Zealand Stock Exchange estimated that between 12 and 15 per cent of the population were share investors, ahead of Australia with eight per cent.

Unfortunately, the local stock market was effectively a giant pyramid scheme of companies built on selling and reselling the same inflated property portfolios, and pipe-dream investments such as angora goat farms. Between 1983 and October 1987, more than 200 companies listed on the New Zealand market. (By comparison, the NZX has had about 40 new listings between 2012 and 2023.)

Naïve Kiwi investors piled into dodgy listed investment firms on a mix of hype and hope. Prior to the crash, one of the most high-profile of these, Brierley Investments, had 160,000 New Zealand shareholders — about five per cent of the population. In an era with no internet, limited disclosure requirements for listed companies and no Takeovers Code, retail investors really were flying blind.

There has never been a clear consensus on what caused the Wall Street plunge. There had been a rapid rise in values that had started to diverge from the fundamentals of the economy. There were growing fears in the US about soaring inflation and interest rates. A correction may have been due, but the scale was unprecedented. The relatively recent arrival of computerised trading platforms has been blamed for exacerbating the big fall.

One thing that isn't in doubt is that it hit New Zealand harder than anywhere else in the world. Our market plunged 15 per cent in a day, initially less than in the US, but that was just the start. Most major markets started bouncing back within weeks. The US economy grew through 1988, and Wall Street was back at pre-crash levels by 1989. But by the end of February 1988, New Zealand's market had fallen almost 60 per cent from its peak. It took years to recover. In fact, on a capital index basis — without factoring in dividends — the local stock exchange has never topped its 1987 peak.

The economy went into recession in 1988 (again) and, perhaps most damaging of all, a generation of investors — the baby boomers — turned away from capital markets and put their savings into property and property-focused finance companies.

Broker, fund manager and financial commentator Brian Gaynor believed the bad experience many had in the 1980s did irreparable damage to the investing mentality of a generation. 'There were an awful lot of people in their twenties and they got [massacred], and so they turned their back on the market,' he opines. 'That's one of the reasons the market has changed and so many people have gone into residential property.'

At the heart of the ideological revolution were Labour's finance minister Roger Douglas and associate finance minister Richard Prebble. The pair were fast shedding any connection to old Labour Party values built on state intervention-controlled capitalism and socialism. Along with Lange and a couple of other energetic young ministers — Mike Moore and Michael Bassett — they were dubbed the Fish and Chip Brigade, after a photo in the *Herald* showed them holding a strategy meeting around a table strewn with greasy paper and a large serving of New Zealand's favourite takeaway. The iconic photo — in which Prebble wasn't actually present — spoke to working-class Labour values, even if the strategy didn't.

Initially, though, as excise taxes and import tariffs came off, working-class Kiwis suddenly had access to better cars, better stereos and snappier clothes that had previously been luxury goods, and it wasn't hard to sell that first wave of consumerism as egalitarian.

The breath of fresh air that the Fourth Labour Government brought to New Zealand was widely embraced, and it killed off a lot of economic division. Collectively, mainstream New Zealand kicked socialism and Keynesian economics to touch. The policies were quickly dubbed Rogernomics, after the finance minister, but with a nod to Reaganomics, the free-market reforms being unleashed in America at the same time.

In a 2023 interview, Douglas told me that there was never really a grand ideological plan that he and his Labour colleagues were following at the time. 'I think it was more organic. We were faced with a problem, we needed to fix it. Had I been tribal in the sense of Labour right or wrong, I don't think we would have necessarily done it.' Rogernomics, he said, was really just a media invention. 'Cabinet was a real mixture of people who decided that they were gonna do the right thing, and if they lost, so be it, but they were gonna do what they thought was right. I don't think we have that any more.'

Later, from the 1990s, Douglas would take the ideology more seriously. But those initial reforms stuck and remain deeply embedded in this country's economic foundations. For some 40 years now, successive New Zealand governments have offered up changes in style and personality, they have turned the fiscal spending up and down, they've been kinder or tougher with welfare; but the open free-market outlook that the Fourth Labour Government pioneered has remained solid.

Both major parties remain supportive of free trade, an independent Reserve Bank, and private ownership of major infrastructure like tele-communications and power. In relative terms (internationally) our taxes remain low, unions remain marginalised. Both major parties take national debt very seriously — running it at much lower levels (as a percentage of GDP) than other comparable nations — and put plenty of store in the judgements and advice of the big financial ratings agencies like Standard and Poor's and Moody's.

Just look at the similarities of the fiscal policies served up by both Labour and National in the 2023 election campaign. Despite the rhetoric around spending and different approaches to tax, the overall numbers were remarkably similar, both promising to get the Crown accounts to surplus by 2026–27 — and both sitting to the economic left of where Douglas and Prebble were taking the government in the late 1980s.

Eventually the Labour Party splintered as the policies of Prebble and Douglas moved the party so far to the right that Lange could no longer tolerate them. He stepped down as prime minister in 1989 after a battle with Douglas over plans to introduce a flat tax rate. Douglas and Prebble would go on to form New Zealand's first hard-line monetarist party, ACT. (No government in New Zealand has ever attempted a policy as radically right-wing as a flat tax. Not even the modern version of ACT, which favours lower taxes generally, sees this as viable in the current political climate.)

In 1989, that internal Labour Party split, and Lange's sacrifice, headed off the flat tax and other more radical plans to take New Zealand's economy down a pure free-market path. But the party never recovered, and after some internal turmoil and two leadership changes, Labour was kicked out of power in 1990. New Zealanders, however, were still keen on free-market reform.

National, under the leadership of affable King Country farmer Jim Bolger and no-nonsense finance minister Ruth Richardson, carried on the programme of reform, selling more assets, and slashing government spending and regulation in a successful attempt to chase down and beat inflation. But the social cost was high, and by the early 1990s unemployment reached levels only surpassed by the worst days of the Great Depression.

As far as we knew as kids of that era, the economy was always bad. The government was always broke, unemployment rising. From the mid-

1980s, the grim local news played out against a backdrop of British pop culture where we heard about the three million unemployed, the miners' strike, and widespread hatred of Margaret Thatcher — all via alternative rock and alternative comedy like *The Young Ones*. It just seemed obvious there would be no work for us in the future. Unemployment was endemic.

CENTRAL GOVERNMENT DEBT
AS A PERCENTAGE OF GDP (2022)*

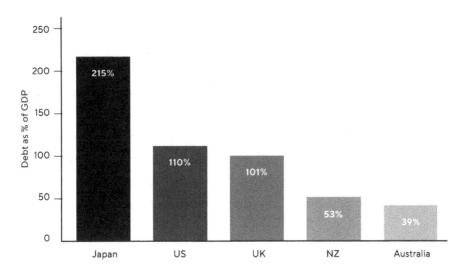

* Gross debt (source: IMF)

Jim Bolger's surf team

Getting the economy back into shape was painful. Ruth Richardson delivered a brutal cost-cutting Budget in 1991 that was aimed at balancing the books and reducing debt. Perhaps it had to be done, but it hit the economy hard. Government departments slashed jobs, people stopped spending, and businesses were forced to cut costs. New Zealand went back into recession and unemployment reached double figures, hitting 10.6 per cent in 1992. For the Māori population, the unemployment rate hit a staggering 26 per cent that year. On top of that, the criteria for claiming a benefit were toughened, and benefit rates were slashed. University fees went up, living allowances were cut and we were introduced to the joys of student loans.

The job market was genuinely terrible when I left university. I kept my eyes peeled for more meaningful work ... but there was none, and I ended up on the dole in 1993, working and studying part time and hanging around the fringes of a burgeoning grunge rock scene. We used to joke about signing on to Jim Bolger's surf team — being state-sponsored layabouts. It sounds kind of cool, but the reality is that after a few months it starts to dent your self-esteem. I found myself getting quite depressed.

Unemployment is bad for mental health, and it can become a dead-end trap for people who don't have the family support and social privilege that I did.

I think my experiences are one of the reasons that, when considering the trade-offs central banks and governments make between running higher inflation or higher unemployment (something called the Phillips curve), I lean towards avoiding recession and unemployment.

UNEMPLOYMENT AND THE KIWI CROCODILE HUNTER

If you had to choose an economist to make a movie about, New Zealander William (Bill) Phillips would be an excellent candidate.[3] (Spoiler alert: by the end of the movie you'll have learned about the relationship between unemployment and inflation.)

Phillips, who was born in 1914 at Te Rehunga near

---

3   If anyone wants to make the movie, feel free to give me a call, but we'll have to give former Reserve Bank governor Alan Bollard a cut of the profits. He wrote the definitive biography in 2016: *A Few Hares to Chase: The Life and Economics of Bill Phillips*.

Dannevirke, was one of those adventurous, number 8 wire inventor types that Kiwi legends are made of. He dropped out of school early and headed to Australia, worked as a crocodile hunter, and travelled to China, where he got caught up in the Japanese invasion and had to escape through Russia.

When he got to the UK, he trained as an electrical engineer and then enlisted in the Royal Air Force at the outbreak of World War Two. He was in Singapore when it fell to the Japanese, but escaped on a troopship to Java. Seemingly a lightning rod for Japanese invasion, he was stuck in Java when it fell, and he ended up being a prisoner of war for three and a half years. While in the prison camp he learned Mandarin from Chinese prisoners, repaired and miniaturised a secret radio, and fashioned a secret water boiler for tea which he hooked into the camp lighting system.

After the war, Phillips was made a Member of the Order of the British Empire (MBE) for his services, and he enrolled at the London School of Economics — where he invented a hydraulic computer in his spare time.

The MONIAC (Monetary National Income Analogue Computer) was literally a mechanical computer that used water flows to model the flow of money through the British economy. The economists at LSE were so impressed with it, they gave him a teaching job. One of his MONIACs is now housed in the excellent museum at the Reserve Bank in Wellington.

But none of that is why Bill Phillips is famous. He is famous for work which inspired a curve, a graph that explicitly described the correlation between unemployment and inflation. It was called the Phillips curve and it revolutionised economics.

It seems intuitive now. If we step back from technical definitions of recession, it's clear that two economic phenomena really ruin lives: unemployment and inflation.

We'll explore pricing and inflation more in the next chapters. But it turns out there is a correlation between inflation and unemployment. When inflation is up, there is more money in the economy, business booms and unemployment falls. When economies slow, inflation falls as demand dries up and businesses have to cut costs — so unemployment rises.

In 1958, Phillips wrote a paper, 'The Relation between Unemployment and the Rate of Change of Money Wage Rates in the United Kingdom, 1861–1957', in which he described the inverse relationship between wage rises and unemployment. In 1960, two other economists took Phillips' work and made explicit the link between inflation and unemployment. In other words, when inflation is high, unemployment is low, and vice versa. They named the curve after Bill.

The Phillips curve underpins the way central banks use their tools — such as interest rates — to try to keep the economy in good shape. Like a lot of mid-twentieth-century economics, it has been subject to a lot of revision. Our old monetarist mate Milton Friedman called the curve into question, suggesting it would hold only in the short term. In the 1970s, the world experienced a bad patch where unemployment and inflation were both high at the same time — suggesting a breakdown in the Phillips curve. We also had a patch in the 2010s when both were low.

But at a basic and intuitive level the Phillips curve still makes sense, especially in the short term. When a central bank needs to bring inflation down, it puts the interest rates up, which removes cash from the economy. Businesses have to cut back; unemployment rises.

Phillips, for the record, headed home to Australia and then back to New Zealand, where he continued as an academic but with a focus on his real passion: Chinese studies. He died in Auckland in 1976.

There's a strong case to be made that the reforms of the early 1990s went too far and the poorest New Zealanders paid too high a price, with social inequality widening and becoming entrenched. By mid-decade the turmoil had settled, at least in terms of the economic trend and the most important statistics. The economy was looking more stable and sustainable. But divisions around the social breakdown and inequality that those reforms unleashed remained, and are still with us.

When I look back on the 1980s, what seems to define the era was our expectation that the economy would always be terrible, and the very real threat of unemployment had a powerful effect on our outlook. But perhaps we were lucky to have been born into an era of low expectations. Maybe the boomers, with that long, golden period of economic growth through their childhood and teens, were set up for years of disappointment as the economy climbed and dipped on a rollercoaster of recession for the next 50 years.

To me, though, having enough jobs to keep the population fully employed and give people a sense of purpose are the most powerful measures of economic success. The cohesion and value that full employment brings to society is still undervalued, especially in an era when we all feel the pain of inflation. The dignity that work brings is esoteric and just one of many things not captured by a strict traditional focus on GDP. If we allow enough people to be unemployed for too long, we see society deteriorate.

If we focus on skills and jobs and keep people working, they will be motivated people and they will find their own path to self-improvement. Better productivity and a wealthier nation will follow. That's why we measure GDP and count recessions. It's a means to an end. The end is about jobs.

But GDP itself is an odd concept. That's what I want to look at next.

Chapter 7

GDP or
not GDP?

Gross national product does not allow for the health of our children, the quality of their education or the joy of their play . . . it measures everything, in short, except that which makes life worthwhile.
— Robert Kennedy, 1968

....

We've looked at booms and busts, the economic ups and downs that shaped our history. But how are we measuring those ups and downs? What's the metric that we use to keep score? The obvious answer is GDP: gross domestic product. If GDP is growing, then the economy is good and we're all happy . . . right?

How much growth is enough to keep us happy? That's a little less clear. Not enough and the economy can stagnate — which may as well be recession (and may well become one if confidence wavers). Too much growth and economies hit limits.

We get inflation and we begin to worry about unsustainable economic bubbles that will go pop. But the economy must grow. We must make more things, do more things, buy and sell more things. That's what the political and economic headlines tell us, day in and day out.

Why do we have to keep growing? For starters, that is the way capitalism incentivises us. It's often called the profit motive, and it's highly effective. Capitalism rewards us for producing better things and more of them. It's a fundamental principle which probably has its roots in evolutionary ideas of competition. Biology hard-wires us to seek advantage.

The profit motive is the idea behind Adam Smith's 'invisible hand': that selfish force that drives rational economic behaviour. The idea has been so successful that humans often forget that we don't always need more. There are limits to how much we can eat, drink and consume. Even if we excel at indulging, we all face a finite time limit. You can't take it with you, so the saying goes, and from an environmental perspective we can see that more is actually bad for us all. But that doesn't seem to stop us chasing more wealth. If someone else has more and we have less, we often feel like we're losing out. It's a bias that capitalism seeks to exploit at every turn.

David Pilling, author of *The Growth Delusion*, describes the way capitalism and economic growth have become an arms race between individuals who are always trying to stay one step ahead of their neighbours. Pilling is obviously no fan of the modern media obsession with GDP and economic growth. Funnily enough, though, even the guy who pioneered the modern notion of GDP in the 1930s didn't buy it himself.

Simon Kuznets, a Russian-born economist who moved to the US in the 1920s, revolutionised and codified the accounting of economic activity. He also devised a theory — called the Kuznets curve — that showed how, as national economic output grew, inequality started to fall. But he was always sceptical about using his measurement system to assess the overall welfare of people. 'The welfare of a nation can scarcely be inferred from a measurement of national income,' he said. 'Distinctions must be kept in mind between quantity and quality of growth, between its costs and return, and between the short and the long term. Goals for more growth should specify more growth of what and for what.'[4]

In other words, we need to get over the idea that growth is good for its

4   Sabastian Hunt, 'The Case Against GDP, Made by Its Own Creator', Gross National Happiness USA, 5 March 2021, https://gnhusa.org/gpi/the-case-against-gdp-made-by-its-own-creator/.

own sake. Kuznets (in typical economist fashion) is suggesting we should do a better job of measuring things and setting targets. We should grow parts of the economy that are good for us and forget about stuff that isn't.

But despite his concerns and hopes, his original GDP idea proved so simple and compelling that it took hold around the world. After all, politicians love compelling, simple ideas (and to be fair, they love them because we all do). To this day, we look to the big macro-economic GDP data from Stats NZ to tell us how the country is doing. GDP has become the de facto scorecard that allows us to view economics like sports and put our national progress on league tables like we were competing for Olympic medals. No wonder it got popular.

Increasingly across the past couple of decades, though, economists have begun to echo Kuznets' concerns about the limits of GDP as a measure, and to question the intense focus we have on it in mainstream politics. Guys like Pilling and French economist Thomas Piketty have had best-sellers pointing this stuff out at great length. With the arrival of Piketty's *Capital in the Twenty-First Century* (2013), and with the GFC still fresh in the memory, it seemed the tide might be turning against the hard-edged focus on GDP growth.

Environmentalists, too, have long been aware that constantly making more and more stuff and calling it progress might have an ecological downside. Perhaps no one did that as profoundly, or with such popular impact, as Dr. Seuss in 1971 with *The Lorax*, which has horrified generations of children with the greedy capitalist the Once-ler and his obsession with business growth (and hopelessly optimistic over-harvesting of truffula trees). In part because of people like Dr. Seuss, we humans have started to acknowledge that the planet's resources are finite.

What's more, there are some big gaps in what GDP measures. Former National Party politician turned academic Marilyn Waring has written extensively on the way GDP is basically sexist, in that it fails to capitalise and value work that is done in the home — traditionally by women — that is clearly of great value to society.

There's a whole bunch of other hugely valuable human activities that GDP largely ignores, like charity work and care for our most vulnerable people. Abstract values like social cohesion and trust are clearly vital to our well-being. There's the black market, the underground economy of sex, drugs and rock'n'roll (well, all the art and music that adds value but never makes money, at least). Let's face it: GDP doesn't actually measure happiness.

So what *does* GDP measure?

Maybe we should cut GDP a break for a moment and consider what it is actually good for. After all, despite the efforts of Piketty et al., we're still using it and arguing about it. Just look at how GDP growth and recession became a political football in the 2023 election.

I'll go to the International Monetary Fund (IMF) for a basic definition: 'GDP measures the monetary value of final goods and services — that is, those that are bought by the final user — produced in a country in a given period of time (say a quarter or a year).' So, basically GDP counts everything that is bought and sold with money. 'It counts all of the output generated within the borders of a country,' the IMF says.[5]

Even if we leave aside the obvious questions that the likes of Waring might raise about that last sentence and just treat GDP as the sum total of economic activity, there are some caveats.

In reality, GDP needs to be looked at on a per capita basis if it is to mean much when we compare countries. Yes, like those Olympic medal tables. We make jokes about per capita tables being lame, because we punch above our weight at the Olympics, but nominal GDP doesn't leave much room for small countries to shine.

For example, China had a nominal annual GDP of about US$18 trillion in 2021, according to Trading Economics (well, according to the Chinese government, really). This represented almost eight per cent of the global

---

5   Tim Callen, 'Gross Domestic Product: An Economy's All', International Monetary Fund, www. imf.org/en/Publications/fandd/issues/Series/Back-to-Basics/gross-domestic-product-GDP.

economy. New Zealand's GDP was about US$250 billion and represented 0.11 per cent of the world economy. Per capita, though, wow, watch out: here come the Kiwis in their black singlets! In 2021, China's GDP per capita was just shy of US$12,000, while New Zealand's was about US$40,000.

But when we look at it that way, what we are getting is an average figure for the wealth of individuals. That might not capture the extent of social inequality that exists. In fact, it doesn't. Regardless, for better or worse, what we tend to focus on is topline GDP growth. What was the percentage by which GDP grew this year compared with the year before? If the economy is growing, we assume that the nation generally is getting wealthier — even if the wealth isn't evenly distributed.

It's the opposite of recession. But even growth can be deceptive. It can be manipulated and created artificially by inflating the money supply — with exactly the kinds of stimulus that central banks have delivered after the GFC and the pandemic: low interest rates and the magic of printing money (quantitative easing).

WHY WE CAN'T JUST PRINT MORE MONEY (AND WHY WE DO ANYWAY)

Why can't we print more money? It's one of the first things children ask when they begin to understand money and ponder being rich and poor.

We can't just print more because money isn't really the same as wealth, of course.

Money is simply a device to measure the value of things. We can't eat it or shelter in it. It's not entertaining or delicious. If we print more, we haven't created any more wealth; we've merely diluted the value of the money. Hence inflation. So far, so simple.

But then, starting with Japan in 2006, followed by the US and Europe after the GFC and almost everyone during the pandemic, central banks decided to print money!

Technically it is called quantitative easing (QE). Even more technically, it is called large-scale asset purchasing (LSAP). Central bankers usually don't like it when the media uses 'money printing' as shorthand for QE. Fundamentally it's a tool central banks use to inject new cash into the economy when other measures — such as cutting interest rates — reach their limits. They do it when we actually need some inflation, when an economy is at risk of stalling and contracting, as it was after the GFC (and as we feared it was during the pandemic).

Here's how it works. The central bank uses its powers to create money to buy government bonds on the secondary market. It can also buy commercial bonds if it needs to really get serious. Actually, if things get bad enough it can buy any assets it wants, but buying bonds makes the most sense.

Central banks don't have to physically print the money; they can just create it electronically. But that isn't the reason why central bankers dislike the term 'money printing'. It's because, while it's true that the cash for all these purchases is magically generated, it's not actually free money. That's because the central bank has to hold the government bonds, or whatever else it's bought, on its balance sheet with a view to selling at a later date and realising the value.

But in the short term, the central bank injects cash into the system because the money that financial institutions get for selling their government bonds on the secondary market didn't exist before.

The central bank's role as a large-scale buyer also puts a cap on government bond yields (keeping rates low) and reassures markets. By reducing the supply of bonds on the market, it encourages investment in other more economically stimulating assets — like company shares.

The Reserve Bank of New Zealand did this to the tune of NZ$53 billion during the pandemic. That's a lot for a small country, but it's small beer compared to US efforts in the past couple of decades. After the GFC (through to 2014), the US Federal Reserve had accumulated US$4.5 trillion of assets via its QE. During the pandemic it purchased roughly another US$2 trillion worth.

Eventually, as noted, those billions and trillions of assets on the central bank balance sheets are supposed to be sold back into the market. Although, given the enormous scale and extended time frames involved — especially in the US — it does all seem a bit like magical printed money.

In the pandemic, as I touched on earlier, we found that the economy didn't shrink as much as expected. The technology and capability of people to keep working from home was better than we thought. So was their ability to keep buying stuff online. With hindsight, it can be seen that we overstimulated the economy. Too much government money was poured into an economy that didn't need it. And it sure did boom.

New Zealand's GDP grew at a whopping 6 per cent in 2021 — although admittedly from the depths of the recessionary slump we had in the initial lockdown of 2020. We weren't really any richer through the pandemic. We weren't creating any more real wealth, but rather we were borrowing and creating the impression of wealth. The GDP data didn't care, though. It just kept telling us we were booming.

We were mostly inflating the economy. It was a reminder that not all growth is good. By the time we got to election year in 2023, the stimulus boom had faded away. The Reserve Bank had raised interest rates to shrink the money supply and slow inflation. Stats NZ data showed the economy declining in the last quarter of 2022 and the first quarter of 2023.

'Recession!' cried opposition political parties. Except it wasn't. The data was revised to show the economy actually managed to hold steady in the first quarter, and it bounced into reasonable growth in the second quarter. Technically speaking, we went into the election with the economy in positive territory. At the time of writing, the debate still wasn't really settled. Record migrant inflows throughout 2023 bolstered top-line GDP growth. But, with a higher population, New Zealand experienced a fall in per capita GDP. In other words, it was still an economy in which many people felt like they were going backwards.

In the end, though, whether we were actually in technical recession or not mattered less than how happy we were feeling about the state of the economy. Not very, was the answer.

The incumbent Labour government lost.

Chapter 8

Don't worry, be happy

*The secret of happiness is not found in seeking
more, but in developing the capacity to enjoy less.
— Socrates*

....

Even prior to Covid-19 and the post-pandemic malaise, it was starting to look like GDP growth wasn't making us very happy any more.

Between 2009 and 2020, New Zealand had an uninterrupted run of economic growth that ranks as the second-longest in our modern history. Only those golden years from 1952 to the late 1960s surpassed it. But the twenty-first-century growth was low and slow. Wages didn't rise much. House prices were booming, making some people much richer but leaving others behind. The real story wasn't nearly as good as the long absence of recession made it look. Something called the Easterlin paradox was at play.

In 2019, I had the privilege of interviewing American professor Richard Easterlin, who by then was a 93-year-old veteran, but still working — and travelling to obscure distant countries like New Zealand. Easterlin was a student of Simon Kuznets — the guy who invented GDP and then warned us not to obsess over it — but he is famous in his own right for his work on GDP. He was the first economist to apply economic discipline to studies of personal happiness.

Easterlin picked up on Kuznets' concerns about GDP as a primary measure of economic well-being, and he developed the new model, the Easterlin paradox. He looked at historic records of economic growth based on GDP against surveys of happiness that had already been carried out by social scientists.

What he found was that, while incomes had more or less doubled over the time, happiness levels hadn't moved. Basically, as countries moved from poor to wealthier, national happiness rose for a while, but there was a point where it plateaued and stopped growing, even as people got wealthier. Adding more wealth no longer added to other measures of personal well-being. It turns out that's got a lot do with the way humans think in terms of social ranking. Easterlin explained it with a question he used to ask his undergraduate students.

Imagine you are graduating, and you have a choice between a salary of $50,000 or $100,000 — with all other aspects of the job being the same. Of course, 100 per cent of people will choose the higher salary. But weirdly, what the research found was that people's decision-making was influenced by what others were offered. When people were asked to choose between a $100,000 salary (but with everyone else making $200,000) or a $50,000 salary (but with everyone else making $25,000), about two-thirds of people chose the lower option.

'What it's showing is that how you feel about what you make depends not only on how big the number is, but also on what others are making,' Easterlin said. 'And the more others are making, the less happy you are. So the explanation is a phenomenon we call social comparison. It's really a phenomenon of relative income, not absolute income.'

This kind of social comparison decision-making is also observed in monkeys. In a 2003 study by researchers Sarah Brosnan and Frans de Waal, capuchin monkeys happily ate either a piece of cucumber or a grape when on their own. But they hurled the cucumber in disgust if it was all they were offered and they saw another monkey getting a grape.

We're still like monkeys in a lot of ways when it comes to money. I'll come back to those capuchins when we look at the price of things.

We can apply this view to our own consumption of the bright shiny things that make us happy. Consider the ever-increasing size of our TV sets, for example. Are we really much happier watching television now than people were with their small, fuzzy screens 50 years ago? Or is the joy that people experienced at having any TV at all, compared with having no TV, impossible to ever surpass?

There appears to be a law of diminishing returns, a happiness curve. There's a point on the curve where, paradoxically, adding economic gain doesn't make us any happier. 'Mo Money Mo Problems,' as rapper Biggie Smalls more famously put it. The paradox raises some fundamental questions about economics. If all our efforts are focused on striving to improve a measure that doesn't raise our overall happiness, then what is the point?

Ultimately, there are three things that are fundamental to happiness, Easterlin said. 'First, people's living conditions – having a job and enough money to live comfortably. Then, good family lives, and third, health.'

I suspect Biggie and his gangsta rap friends might have added a couple of other things to that list. But you get the idea. This is starting to sound like old-fashioned common sense.

THE LAW OF MARGINAL UTILITY (OR WHY YOU SHOULDN'T EAT THREE ICE-CREAMS)

Some economic concepts seem so basic, you can't quite believe they had to be invented. The law of marginal utility is a bit like that. It's a companion to the law of supply and demand and describes the way our demand for something changes depending on our relationship to it. Let's leap straight to an absurd example to illustrate the economics of utility.

Consider how much you'd pay for a bottle of water if you were lost in the desert and dying of thirst. The answer is: a lot. Depending on how near death you were, it might even be worth everything you own. Now imagine you're in a boat on a freshwater lake in a torrential downpour. That bottle of water has almost no utility. It's worthless. You're actually looking for less water in your life.

It doesn't seem like rocket science to point out that economic value is relative. In fact, it's probably kind of intuitive and built into the way humans have always gathered and traded resources. But standing back, naming and analysing something that seems intuitive is what social scientists do.

Understanding something like marginal utility is helpful when we try to build a more complex model of how an economy works. Without factoring it into the demand side of the equation, supply and demand curves will always be off-kilter.

A lot of philosophers and early economists touched on the idea of marginal utility in their work. They applied a similar theory to the supply side of the economic equation, helping manufacturers understand economies of scale (or diminishing marginal cost). But it wasn't until the late nineteenth century that marginal utility was widely applied to price setting and consumer behaviour.

Ice-cream is a well-worn example used to illustrate what the 'marginal' bit means in marginal utility. I like it because I am weak-willed when it comes to ice-cream, but feel free to imagine potato chips or whatever works for you in your example.

You might happily pay for an ice-cream on a hot summer's day. You might enjoy the first one so much you go back for a second. But that second ice-cream will never be quite as good — or as valuable — as the first. It's pretty good, though, and it still adds some pleasure to your day. So, while the marginal utility of the second ice-cream is diminished, it is still *positive*.

How about a third ice-cream? Perhaps the ice-cream seller had a 'three for $10' deal, so you figure, why not, it's basically free. But you don't really enjoy that third ice-cream because you're getting full. That third ice-cream can be said to have *zero* marginal utility. In fact, now you think about it, it made you feel a bit sick and also a bit guilty (you were supposed to be watching your weight). So actually, that third ice-cream had *negative* marginal utility.

In a fit of self-loathing, you realise you never should have bought the third ice-cream; you're a foolish, greedy pig and it was a terrible economic mistake.

In fact, that kind of pricing model — encouraging you to buy more units of food or drink despite their diminishing marginal utility — is all too common with fast-food chains. That's because of the diminishing marginal costs at their end. After all, the fixed cost of filling that box of fries is much the same for a small one as for an extra-large. They've already heated up the deep-fryer. The labour cost changes by only one additional hand movement (which shouldn't trouble the teenager serving you). The potatoes have already been prepared. The extra cost of adding 25 per cent more fries is so small, they might as well discount them heavily as an incentive for you to consume more.

It's the same with the extra-large cola at the movies. There's no point buying the small one, since the last 250ml on the large is basically free — so you may as well have too much cola. And the special 'meal deal' has made the popcorn so cheap you'd be mad to just get the drink. If only you had an economist there to remind you that you'll be feeling sick by the end of the cup, the salty popcorn will have burned the surface off your tongue, and you'll need to run to the loo right before the final showdown in that four-and-a-half-hour Marvel movie.

We should probably all think a bit more about marginal utility in our daily economic lives. If we did, we might be healthier and happier and have a few extra dollars in our pocket. Which is a good reminder that just because an idea is simple or basic, that doesn't mean it isn't relevant and important.

Recognising that happiness is relevant to economics and integrating it into the discipline is no small thing, though. Easterlin's work has gained a lot of traction down the years, but it was quite radical when he started it in the early 1970s.

The notion of 'well-being' has been adopted as a broader measure by several governments, including our own. In the UK, the statistics department now regularly measures public happiness. In New Zealand, under the advice of Finance Minister Grant Robertson, the 2017 Labour government was the first in the world to pass legislation putting well-being at the centre of the Treasury's work on economic management.

Obviously, I'm in favour of the progress towards adopting a broader, more holistic view of economic growth. I think that's a no-brainer. All economic data needs to be contextualised before we start taking it seriously and acting on it. But I do want to argue that there's still a place for the old-school measurement of GDP, more or less in the way Kuznets did it.

As a measure of capitalism in action, GDP captures many — though not all — of the things we do that create wealth and enhance life. It is good at measuring technological progress, for example. It measures the houses we build, the cars we manufacture, the beer we drink and the movies we watch. It basically reflects all the biases and imperfections of capitalism. And as long as we're going to keep using a capitalist system, it seems important to keep track of it. We do need to count how many more widgets we've made and sold this year compared with last. That's a basic piece of economic accounting that dates to the ancient Babylonians recording the size of their harvests.

Yet, maybe GDP doesn't need to be so central to our idea of a successful economy. We do need to recognise the way different groups and individuals are experiencing the same economic cycle. Perhaps, surprisingly, a long economic boom can be a tough time for people on fixed incomes. Inflation often takes hold, and the cost of living can rise, so it costs more to get things done in a boom than in a recession. Interest rates start to rise, and if you are not benefiting directly from the boom times, then you are losing. Stuck in your own little micro-recession, you just feel worse if all the world is talking about the great times unfolding while you go backwards.

Conversely, a recession can be good news, so long as you don't lose your job. Economists get that. So do politicians. US President Harry Truman allegedly once said: 'It's a recession when your neighbour loses his job; it's a depression when you lose yours.' It might be an apocryphal quote, but it's a nice folksy way of making the point that we all experience a downturn differently.

I think one of the reasons we need to retain a focus on classic GDP growth is because when growth disappears, we need to know when and why and how to fix it. GDP growth might not make us happier in the long run, but major recessions mean large-scale job losses, and losing your job will make you unhappy (if I haven't already stressed that enough).

People have a bad habit of taking the good times for granted until they are gone. And once the boom times are over, we suddenly feel nostalgic for a golden age.

EARTHQUAKES, PANDEMICS AND BROKEN WINDOWS

There's another annoying quirk in the way we use GDP to measure economic progress. When bad things happen and stuff gets destroyed, that costs money. And the way we measure growth means that sometimes after a disaster, such as an earthquake or flood, all the rebuilding activity can seem like a positive thing. The nineteenth-century French economist Frédéric Bastiat first called out this fallacy with a parable about a baker whose son breaks a window, leading to an economic boost for the glazier. It's now known in economics as the broken window fallacy.

In Bastiat's day there were even economic arguments made for war — that it could stimulate activity and generate wealth. Moral issues aside, that might hold if your idea of war is just conquering another nation and taking all their wealth. But as a means of stimulating an economy, war offers limited upside.

Waging war in and of itself is obviously a cost. Sometimes disasters or wars happen at times when economies are already in the doldrums. When that happens, the boost from increased military production can stimulate economic recovery. On paper, for instance, the US benefited from World War Two because it brought the terrible austerity of the Great Depression to an end. There was postwar economic growth as governments invested in rebuilding the world. But the real economic cost was vast.

More often than not, the myth that disasters and wars create growth derives from the fact that we borrow to fund them or repair things afterwards. Because the need suddenly seems urgent, we take on huge debts, as New Zealand did through the pandemic in 2020 and 2021. But in doing so, we just displace the immediate costs of the bad event and spread them across time. Sometimes after a disaster, insurance companies cover a lot of the immediate costs. But you can bet we eventually pay the price for that too, as premiums rise over time.

Meanwhile, what is far easier to see is that construction activity picks up and jobs are created. GDP numbers for the economic quarter immediately after a disaster might show strong economic growth. So, if you just looked at short-term data, you could be forgiven for thinking the disaster was good news.

Bastiat's point, made in his essay 'That Which We See and That Which We Do Not See', was that we need to step back and look at the big picture. We need to see the impact on the whole economy over time. If we do that, suddenly it seems obvious that endlessly breaking things and repairing them is no way to get rich.

Chapter 9

Work smarter, not harder

Productivity is being able to do things
that you were never able to do before.
— Franz Kafka

....

One way to find out whether GDP growth is really making us wealthier and more prosperous is to look under the hood. We can dig into production statistics to see whether they justify the topline growth number. We call this productivity. It's something you'll hear politicians and economists talk about a lot because (spoiler alert) we have a bit of a problem with it in this country.

Boats, baches and New Zealand's productivity problem

How productive were you today? We all have good days and bad, I guess. Businesses can be like that, and so can entire economies.

When we talk about productivity in economics (and we do talk about it a lot) we basically just mean the amount of output that can be produced with a given set of inputs. Say a factory with 100 workers can make 1000 widgets a day. The productivity rate is 10 widgets per worker. If you add 10 workers and get 1100 widgets, that's not a productivity increase, because we've just increased the inputs and output has risen in proportion.

But let's say we decide to improve the mind-set of the workers. Maybe we play nice music throughout the day and put on a special lunch. If the same 100 workers were more motivated, they might produce 1100 widgets in a day, meaning the productivity rate has improved.

The boss might be happy with that, but it could also just be that everyone is working harder, which ultimately is not necessarily a sustainable way to boost productivity. How about if the boss adds a new computerised logistics system that measures worker performance? It crunches the data and figures out some workers are better at building the frames for the widgets and some are better at finishing them off. Now they can optimise the workflow in the factory. Suddenly the same 100 workers are producing 1200 widgets a day. That's a real productivity gain — the kind we want to achieve across an economy.

When economic growth slows, governments can legislate for higher minimum wages, or central banks cut interest rates to boost the amount of money in circulation, and, as we've covered earlier, these measures can inflate GDP growth. But inflation doesn't make anybody richer. We don't collectively get any wealthier in real terms unless we work harder or work smarter and produce more stuff.

The other unproductive way we can drive growth is by just working more, as noted in the example above. Technically that can create real wealth, but at some point it starts to undermine our quality of life — which, as Richard Easterlin pointed out, kind of defeats the purpose of economic growth.

There's a reason we talk a lot about working smarter, not harder. Unfortunately, the reason is that we're terrible at it in New Zealand. A lot of our economic growth in the past two decades has been down to working harder. Governments (of all stripes) worry about it a lot, and in 2010 an independent Crown entity, the New Zealand Productivity Commission, was set up to try and improve things. It has been a struggle, to say the least.

Research by the Productivity Commission for the year to March 2020 (just pre-dating the pandemic) showed New Zealanders work 34.2 hours per week, compared with 31.9 hours in other OECD countries. And New Zealanders produced less, achieving only $68 of output per hour, compared with $85 in other OECD countries.

'Poor productivity results in higher prices for everyday items, which can impose a larger burden on those with low incomes,' the report concluded. 'When productivity growth is lower, wage growth tends to be lower too, meaning some families struggle to make ends meet. The result is they work longer hours and have less time . . . with family [and the community].'[6]

There is broad political consensus about the need to improve productivity and grow higher-value sectors, such as technology. Politicians of all varieties will fall back on it as a solution to problems like paying off the nation's debt. That's not surprising when the other two solutions are spending less or taxing more. But it seems neither Labour nor National has ever had an appetite for the dramatic policy shifts that economists suggest might shift the productivity dial.

The irony is that most of the things we highlight as drivers of better productivity sound like common-sense policies we all agree on. That's why they are such perennial talking points for the politicians.

On the 2023 election campaign trail I asked both (then) finance minister Grant Robertson and his challenger, National's Nicola Willis, to give me their number one solution to New Zealand's productivity issue. They both opted out, saying that it was about investing more in a whole bunch of things — most of which they agreed on. Here's a loose but familiar list of all the things politicians and experts cite as ways to improve economic productivity:

• **Investment in education and skills:** We obviously do that, to a point. New Zealand ranks pretty well globally for its education system, and broadly the population has the basics of literacy and numeracy. We're also good at producing creative thinkers with a broad-based curriculum that's heavy on the arts. But we could do with more engineers and scientists and computer software developers. Part of

6   'New Zealanders Working Harder, Not Smarter — Productivity Report', RNZ, 27 May 2021, https://tinyurl.com/mry5zznv.

the education puzzle is training people with the right skills for all the tech that drives economic growth.

- **Research and development:** This is a big one where New Zealand lags behind other, more productive nations. According to Stats NZ, our R&D expenditure as a proportion of GDP rose from 1.46 per cent to 1.47 per cent between 2020 and 2022 — heading in the right direction at least. But the average for OECD nations was 2.7 per cent for the same period. And most of the highly productive nations we say we'd like to emulate spend a much higher proportion than that. Israel tops the table at 5.5 per cent, South Korea 4.9 per cent, Germany, Japan and Sweden all above three per cent. R&D investment leads to new products and even whole new industries, or it drives the development of new processes or tools to do the stuff we already do more efficiently.

- **Access to capital:** We need to ensure that businesses have access to affordable capital so they can invest in R&D and new technology. A well-functioning financial system can help encourage investment in productivity-enhancing technologies and equipment. Unfortunately, as we'll note in more detail in later chapters, New Zealand has a love affair with property investment. With most of our investment capital tied up in property, we invest less into the local share market and other areas like venture capital, private equity and start-up funds that can accelerate growth for smart businesses. Our banks also prefer to lend for property investment than business investment, so borrowing to fund the latter is not easy.

- **Tax incentives and government subsidies:** Some people argue that government should incentivise business investment in R&D and productivity-enhancing equipment. That's something that can be done directly with grants or indirectly with subsidies and tax breaks. In fact, we do both in New Zealand, but not as generously as business would like. Whether we should lean harder into low tax or offer grants probably depends on your political views on the efficiency of government. In fact, that debate can be applied to the entire tax system. How much tax is too much? Lower taxes help businesses thrive and economies become more productive. That's a debate that's never really been settled (see the Laffer curve, page 178).

- **Streamline regulations:** As we saw in the look back at life in the 1970s, over-regulating the economy is a good way to stifle innovation, growth and productivity. It's a question of balance, of course. Business groups are always opposed to red tape — but we do need some rules to protect worker rights and safety. We need to ensure businesses aren't benefiting at the expense of the wider community by polluting or drawing too heavily on natural resources. We also need to regulate against monopolies. Competition generally encourages efficiency and innovation, leading to higher productivity levels. We'll look more closely at that issue in the next chapter on pricing.

- **Infrastructure development:** The most productive nations have excellent infrastructure to keep the economy moving at pace. Whether it's roads or rail, internet connections or the power grid, investing in infrastructure projects can reduce costs and improve efficiency. Just imagine how much time and money traffic jams cost in wasted output. Actually, you don't have to imagine. A 2017 study by the NZ Institute of Economic Research estimated that traffic congestion in Auckland alone was costing the economy $3.5 million every day, or around $1.3 billion a year.[7] High-speed rail network, anyone? As a geographically challenging country with a small population, New Zealand faces some big decisions around funding infrastructure.

  There's a case that governments should borrow more to invest in infrastructure, which will pay off in time with productivity gains. But many people worry about the ability of government to deliver big public projects efficiently.

- **Entrepreneurship:** After years of debating why New Zealand lags behind the rest of the OECD, some economists have even suggested

---

7   Susan Edmunds, 'Traffic Congestion Costs Auckland's Economy $1.3b a Year: Report', *Stuff*, 3 August 2017, www.stuff.co.nz/business/95383973/traffic-congestion-costs-aucklands-economy-13b-a-year-report.

we lack the entrepreneurial culture seen in other nations, such as the US. We don't have enough self-made millionaires (or billionaires). It's even been suggested that those who do succeed in business are too laid-back and have a 'bach, boat and BMW' mind-set. In other words, our businesspeople and entrepreneurs strive for the good life but, having achieved it, tend to cash up rather than drive their business on to large-scale success.

Maybe we're just a chilled-out island nation that doesn't want to be the new Singapore or the Switzerland of the South Pacific. Fair enough. But that doesn't mean we can't be better at business in our own distinct Kiwi style. We can still do more to create an environment that supports entrepreneurship. This can include building it into the school curriculum, and supporting more business incubators, mentorship programmes and funding opportunities for start-ups.

- **A more inclusive economy:** Consider how much potential economic growth is being lost because of structural social inequalities. Kids that go to primary school hungry are less likely to make it through to university. We often consider the costs of all those young people lost to the system — committing crime, living on the streets or joining gangs. We worry about expenditure on benefits and policing and prison costs. But there's also an opportunity cost. If these people were educated and contributing to the economy they'd be adding to our collective wealth. We should keep trying to make serious progress on social inequity and poverty. We should do it because it is fair and right — but if that isn't enough, we should also be incentivised by the added economic value it would deliver to us all.

Well, there's no doubt that improving a nation's productivity is a complex and continuous process that requires a combination of policies, investments and cultural changes. Robertson and Willis were right. There is no single silver bullet solution. But I wouldn't mind seeing a government picking a big one — like R&D or infrastructure — and really targeting some meaningful change.

Chapter 10

What's up with the price of cheese? Why prices won't sit still

Money often costs too much.
— Ralph Waldo Emerson

....

Why is cheese so expensive? I mean, we make tonnes of the stuff — right?

That's a perennial Kiwi economics question. And the simple answer to that big question about price is the law of supply and demand. On a very deep level that is as close to a perfect answer as we get in economics. But perhaps a better question is this: why do Kiwis care so much about the price of cheese?

In this chapter, I want to look at the storm of social and economic influences that swirl around that law, shaping it and distorting the prices we pay in our daily lives. From the regular ups and downs of filling the car with petrol, the eye-catching specials at the supermarket or the premium we pay for fashionable brands, what drives supply and what causes demand?

The price of things is one of the big forces in our lives. Price decides where we get to live and how we get to live. It decides how we dress, what we drive and what we eat. We might try not to, but we often end up defining ourselves with decisions about price — what we can afford, or what we choose to indulge in. Price provides answers to questions about what we really want and how badly we want it.

So, let's acknowledge that the law of supply and demand is always with us, but it doesn't exist in a vacuum. Demand is driven by human needs and wants, and it starts with our biology: food, warmth, comfort, love, sex. These needs are so intrinsic that understanding their value seems hard-wired into our brains.

Studies have shown that even animals can barter and negotiate a price. Let's return to our simian friends, the capuchin monkeys. In 2005, suspecting that deal-making might be going on in the wild in ways we couldn't recognise, researchers ran an experiment in which they successfully introduced currency to a group of capuchin monkeys. The study, by Yale economist Keith Chen and psychologist Laurie Santos, involved training the monkeys to trade silver discs for food. In no time at all the monkeys were trading for food and responding to price signals, like buying more grapes when they were offered bargain prices.

They even started doing something that revealed they understood the concept of currency as a transferable token. Taking things beyond a straight swap for food, they reinvented the world's oldest profession. The researchers observed a male monkey paying for sex with a silver disc, which the female recipient exchanged afterwards for grapes. The monkey prostitution ethically troubled the researchers, so they took steps to avoid encouraging it further, but it didn't stop them from introducing gambling games with their silver discs.

The monkeys became compulsive gamblers to an extent that became economically irrational — something the researchers ended up realising was more like human behaviour than not. In fact, it prompted Chen to conclude the data made them 'statistically indistinguishable from most stock-market investors'.[8] Perhaps our ability to negotiate our price is both innate and innately flawed.

Of course, while our brains might be hard-wired in similar ways to our primate cousins, we as humans have made great intellectual and cultural leaps, and what we need and want is shaped by our technology. In human evolution, survival of the fittest quickly became survival of the tech-savvy.

---

8   Stephen J. Dubner and Steven D. Levitt, 'Monkey Business', *New York Times*, 5 June 2005, www.nytimes.com/2005/06/05/magazine/monkey-business.html.

There's a good reason nerd culture has survived 100,000 years of violent alpha male-dominated history. Technology is what creates advantage for humans.

It can also convey social status. Since the invention of wheels, we've sought faster, more efficient and better-looking ways to ride on them. An old Toyota Corolla station wagon and a new Porsche 911 will both get you from A to B with a similar degree of ease and comfort. Why does one cost 30 times more than the other? The sporty Porsche is technically much faster — but not really, not on a busy modern road where we all face the same congestion and speed limits. It's more beautifully designed — but not if you have to get three kids to two different football fields with a dog in the back. Let's face it, a sports car is a status symbol, and its practical shortcomings just highlight the indulgence of owning one. (It probably isn't particularly fuel-efficient either.)

Petrol costs are a good reminder that prices are also set by the geopolitical forces that shape the world. Governments, corporations, warlords, oligarchs and billionaires all exert influence on price. Natural resources are controlled and allocated by these big forces. Wars are fought over water and food, or oil and gold. Deals are done between nations to control supply and set prices. Or to open new markets and release demand.

Then there is money itself — hard currency. Some currencies, such as the US dollar, have more value than others. That affects price. The richest economies in the world tend to set the price for money and, by default, the price of everything else. There are financial markets that keep the price of currencies in check, and there are global rules we agree to that empower central banks to control the supply of money and to try and keep prices stable.

Inflation, deflation . . . all the 'flations

Day to day, the nominal price we pay for things rises and falls due to phenomena we collectively describe as inflation (or deflation). This is important at a structural level, for a healthy economy, and at a more basic consumer level — because rising prices suck.

We keep tabs on inflation (or our statistics department does) by recording prices for a set basket of consumer items and measuring how they change on a monthly, quarterly and annual basis. The basket is meant to be a reflection of what we typically buy on a regular basis, and it changes through time. On that basis the index makes a nice time capsule for historians. When it was reviewed and updated in 2020, for instance, vapes were added and CDs were dropped. Reflecting pandemic trends, food and alcohol were upweighted and the weighting of travel fell.[9] Our basket is hypothetical, and not a perfect tool, but it does a good job of showing us inflationary trends.

Inflation and money supply crop up a lot throughout this book. They run through the heart of economics. And we can't really talk about prices without looking at inflation in more detail.

When it comes to rising shopping bills, inflation is the villain of the piece. Although, as we've seen with the myriad influences on pricing, inflation isn't really a price setter. It's a price changer. Inflation is more specifically an influence on the value of money. It steals value from you by diminishing the purchasing power of the cash in your hand.

Of course, nominal prices rise when inflation takes hold because businesses have to lift them to cover the higher input costs they face. Then workers need higher wages to cover their living costs, which adds more costs to business, and up go those prices again. That's what we call an inflationary spiral.

All things being equal, inflation could change the nominal price of things without changing their value much. So long as your wages were going up in sync with the cost of living, the numbers might get bigger, but you wouldn't get any more or less wealthy. Unfortunately, inflation is never quite so fair. It hits different parts of the economy differently at different times, often exaggerating inequalities and eroding trust in the

---

9   Consumer price index review: 2020, Stats NZ, www.stats.govt.nz/methods/consumers-price-index-review-2020.

monetary system, which tends to be based on the price stability of money.

To accept a dollar in exchange for your stuff, you have to be sure that that dollar will still be able to buy roughly the same amount of stuff tomorrow or next week. If inflation is so bad that a dollar loses value in the space of a day or a week, we call that hyperinflation.

Hyperinflation is a specific economic term for the complete meltdown of a monetary system. It relates to prices increasing at rates like 1000 per cent a year, or 50 per cent every month, or some other insanely unsustainable number. It's what happened in Germany in the 1920s. The price of a loaf of bread went from 250 marks in January 1923 to 200 trillion in November (yes, trillion; that's not a typo). There were stories of people burning banknotes to keep warm. It's the extreme example of why we can't let inflation keep spiralling in an economy – and, it almost goes without saying, it caused political upheaval in Germany that led to a world war and some of the greatest atrocities in human history.

Bear in mind that, these days, we get very upset if inflation goes above five per cent a year. Central banks aim for nice, slow inflation that ensures stability and allows maximum economic growth and wealth creation without causing everything to go pop. Good inflation is generally considered to be around two per cent per annum. Most central banks target that, or (like our Reserve Bank) they aim for a band of one to three per cent.

So, hyperinflation is a disaster and can make for a terrible mess – but regular old high inflation isn't great either, as New Zealanders who lived through the value-destroying days of the 1970s–80s will recall. Between 1970 and 1990, inflation never fell below five per cent in New Zealand. It averaged 13 per cent from 1974 to 1987 and peaked at 17 per cent in 1980. People got very sick of inflation, and since the mid-1980s central banks have been empowered to act independently of government and maintain strict control of the money supply. Since it was introduced in 1999, the Reserve Bank of New Zealand has done that with a tool that we call the Official Cash Rate (OCR).

WHAT EVEN IS THE OCR?

Most people get that the Official Cash Rate (OCR) is an interest rate. It features prominently in news reports about the economy, and the Reserve Bank gets to move it up and down every six weeks or so amid much media excitement. But what is it exactly and how does it work? As a working definition, we're just talking about central banks having a state-sanctioned monopoly on the wholesale price for lending and borrowing money. That is why the rate that the Reserve Bank sets is called the official one. It's the baseline interest rate, the starting point for banks before they add their own margins.

This is where it gets more technical. The big commercial banks hold accounts with the Reserve Bank, and these accounts are used to settle transactions at the end of the day. When you buy something, there's usually a transaction between two commercial banks that needs to be settled. The accounts with the Reserve Bank are used to cover transactions that haven't yet been matched up at the end of the day. In fulfilling that function, the Reserve Bank can both charge and pay interest. And by doing that at the lowest available domestic rate, it effectively sets the floor for all other domestic interest rates. So, the level where a central bank decides to set its official rate for an economy has a direct influence on the rate at which banks can lend and borrow.

Every six weeks or so, the Reserve Bank makes a very public decision about where it will set the rate. The drama of this decision creates such a hot news event that these rate decisions are now central to the cycle of economic news. Will the Reserve Bank cut the rate or raise it? Or leave it the same? It all depends on how the economy is tracking.

If things are booming and inflation is becoming a problem, then the rate goes up to increase costs for borrowers. That pushes mortgage rates up and suddenly there is less money circulating in the economy. If the economy is in recession or is growing very slowly, central banks cut rates to encourage more borrowing. If the OCR drops, mortgage rates usually follow. That's good news for homeowners, as it effectively puts cash back in their pockets. It's bad news for savers.

But that's part of the way that interest rates control inflation. When rates are high it encourages saving, which is deflationary. When rates are low it encourages spending, which is inflationary. That's why rates were slashed so radically after demand collapsed in the GFC of 2008 and when lockdowns were imposed in 2020. And it's why they soared in 2022 as inflation started to bite.

Another reason we care about the OCR is the effect local interest rates have on the international value of our currency. Investors who can move money around the world tend to prefer countries with higher interest rates — as long as they're politically stable. So, when the OCR goes up, so does our dollar, and when it goes down, the dollar generally follows.

For an export-led economy like New Zealand, this can be important for commodity prices (not to mention your upcoming overseas holiday). But the Reserve Bank's control is limited around currency. International currency markets are huge. The US dollar dominates, and so it is the US Federal Reserve that has most influence over the global money supply. I see OCR decisions as a barometer of the economy: they send a clear message to the world about where New Zealand is at in the economic circle of life.

Economists and central banks try to keep a handle on what a normal or 'neutral' rate looks like. In other words, how high the OCR should be during times when the economy is nicely balanced. The decisions they make are quite political, since different settings benefit different people in society. Older people are often savers looking for a decent interest rate on bank deposits. Younger people are more likely to have debt — especially if they want to own a home. It helps to look at the historical average. Since the OCR was introduced in 1999, it has averaged 3.84 per cent. Two big events (the GFC and the pandemic) have pushed down that average — and probably our expectations of what a neutral rate should be.

In the post-pandemic years, inflation has been on the rise again, sparking fears of a return to the era of deeply embedded inflation we saw in the 1970s–80s. That's seen central banks lifting interest rates after years at low levels.

Ironically, the banks themselves played a big part in creating that inflation. When the pandemic hit in 2020, economists assumed border closures and lockdowns would crush consumer demand and destroy business the way the GFC had. So, they slashed rates and stimulated the economy. As I've said earlier, it turned out we were better at working and shopping from home than they realised. All the stimulus of cheap borrowing and emergency government spending was too much and it stoked inflation.

One of the reasons economists and central banks got it wrong was that we hadn't seen a global pandemic in 100 years. We had no modern model for what to do. This is a very quick summary of a scenario that still causes a lot of debate and has many more complicated threads to it. I'm not going to jump into the debate about New Zealand's Covid-19 response here. But another reason policymakers may have been too relaxed about inflation risk during the pandemic is that we had started to believe that inflation might be dead.

Through the 1990s a combination of aggressive central bank inflation-targeting, big productivity gains as the world embraced computing, and falling oil prices saw inflation fall sharply. That ushered in an era of ultra-low interest rates (and very cheap borrowing).

In the years after the GFC, the world found itself battling something called deflation.

In New Zealand we had low interest rates, petrol was cheaper than it had been for years, and the free trade deal with China brought a wave of low-cost imported consumer goods, from clothing to camping gear and outdoor furniture. And technology just kept getting cheaper (and smaller). What could economists possibly have had to complain about? Well...

Why falling prices are bad news

Deflation means the value of a dollar is rising too fast instead of falling. It effectively means the price of things is going down. Of course, the idea that falling prices are a bad thing seems counterintuitive. But the problem is that when people expect prices to fall, this can create a recessionary spiral.

The expectation that things will become cheaper suppresses consumer spending and business investment. As consumers, we start to realise that we may as well wait to buy stuff later as it will cost less in the future. As business owners, we have no incentive to expand because, as prices fall, our margins are squeezed and profits fall. The two feed off each other as lower consumption forces businesses to contract and focus on costs. They end up having to cut staff and that causes unemployment to rise (see the Phillips curve, page 82). As unemployment rises, consumer spending falls further — a cheaper TV set or overseas holiday doesn't look so good if you've been laid off — and down we go in a deflationary spiral.

Japan has been the poster child for deflation in the 2000s. With a kick-start from the US, the nation boomed after the war as it concentrated on manufacturing and electronics. From the 1960s to the 1980s, its GDP grew by an average of about six per cent a year. The scale of its economic expansion even started to threaten the US — at least psychologically. (The fear of a Japanese economic takeover is illustrated by the futuristic, Japanese-influenced version of Los Angeles in the 1982 sci-fi classic *Blade Runner.* At that time, the rise and rise of the Japanese economy seemed like a historic inevitability.) But Japan's aging population (older people tend to be savers, not spenders) and a long period of deflation through the 1990s put paid to the country's economic miracle.

In the twenty-first century, the rest of the world has started to see signs of the same problems. Deflation became such an issue in the 2010s that it seemed that people thought the old rules around inflation might have changed. Central banks were so worried about deflation that some of them began cutting official cash rates into negative territory. In the US, Europe and New Zealand the official cash rate was cut to near zero, which meant rates got so low that central banks had nowhere else to go but negative if further cuts had been needed.

It actually happened in Japan, Switzerland and Denmark. Yes, that's as weird as it sounds. If an interest rate is negative, it means, theoretically, that the lender is paying the borrower to take the money. So, you pay the bank to look after your money and, even weirder, the bank pays you to take theirs. In reality it isn't quite so simple. Most of the weirdness in places like Denmark happened at a wholesale level — i.e. between the central bank and the commercial banks.

Research by the New Zealand Treasury concluded that, while banks remain willing to deposit funds at the central bank when the policy rate is negative, they are reluctant to let retail corporate or household interest rates turn negative. In other words, retail banks would probably have to wear the costs of the negative rates in their lending margins just to keep their business sane, and they'd likely make up the difference by charging higher fees.

THE SPEED OF MONEY

We need to look at quantity theory, or the equation $MV = PQ$.

No, wait, don't turn the page! I hate equations with letters in them, too. They feel like the scary maths I dropped out of in high school. (It's amazing how far good arithmetic and understanding percentages can take you in a newsroom; you'll be treated like some kind of nerdy professor.) Real economics has much more complex equations in it that I don't pretend to understand.

I was having a chat with a senior investment banker about how economically illiterate most people are. He told a story about speaking to a university class that didn't even know $MV = PQ$. Ha, imagine that! I laughed and dug desperately into the far reaches of my brain to try and recall what the letters stood for. Then I went back to the office and googled.

I decided I'd better include in the book this one equation, which relates to the speed (or velocity) of money. It's an interesting idea. The equation, otherwise known as the quantity theory of money, is one of the fundamental building blocks of monetarism (the supply-side ideas of Milton Friedman and co.). It is widely accepted as a fact in classical macro-economic theory and, like Einstein's famous $E = MC^2$, $MV = PQ$ is mind-blowing in its own way. Let's break it down.

We've already seen how the amount of money in an economy will affect economic growth: more money means more growth, but can also lead to inflation if it's not backed by productivity gains and real wealth creation. The 'extra for experts' bit in this equation is the velocity of money . . . the V. That's the speed at which money circulates around the economy. In even more basic terms, it is how fast we're spending it.

This is an important part of the equation if we want to build a realistic model of how healthy and vibrant an economy is. When economies are weak, people lose confidence and hoard cash. The V part of the equation slows. So, there is a direct correlation between the amount of money, the speed at which it's circulating and the overall activity (or GDP) of an economy.

The P represents the price of things. The Q represents the quantity of output in the economy. Together they represent the value and volume of the stuff we are collectively producing. So, PQ is basically our GDP.

The equation is telling us that the amount of money (M) in an economy, multiplied by the speed at which the money is circulating (V), will always be equal to nominal GDP — the price of things (P) times the amount of things (Q). Both sides of the equation are always equal, and we can work out one variable if we know the others. If we want to know how fast money is circulating, we can work backwards and divide GDP (PQ) by the total supply of money.

Of course, it all gets much more complicated when you start plugging real numbers in and accounting for variables in those numbers. But let's leave that to the real economists. At the very least, understanding the theory of the equation is helpful if you want to understand how central banks look at the economy . . . and you can use it if you're ever in a conversation where you need to pretend you know about economics.

The sweet spot for prices

Since the reforms of the 1980s, the goal for central banks is to maintain stability with inflation ticking over at between one and three per cent. Why that magic target band?

There's actually no widely agreed reason for this. It just feels right. It does suggest that on balance a deflationary economy is probably worse than a mildly inflationary one. We want to create an environment that is conducive to growth and wealth creation. It also gives central banks some room to cut rates if we get another big financial shock — like a war pushing oil prices up or a share market crash.

Another issue with leaving rates too low for too long is that it encourages too much borrowing. It fuels investment bubbles. How? Low interest rates make savings accounts look like bad value, which in turn can make share market investment overly attractive . . . causing speculative bubbles.

Equity markets love low interest rates because they encourage

INFLATION THROUGH THE YEARS

(Source: Reserve Bank of New Zealand, https://www.rbnz.govt.nz/monetary-policy/about-monetary-policy/inflation)

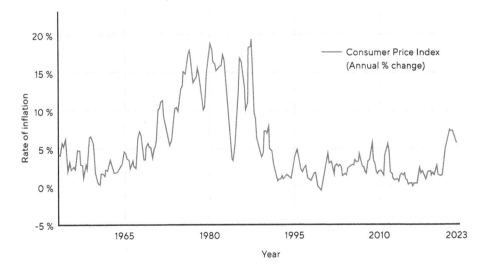

investment in companies that can borrow and expand. We saw this effect during the pandemic when the Reserve Bank slashed interest rates. Money poured into the stock market. From a low point in March 2020, when we were at the height of Covid-19 panic, the local NZX50 soared in value by almost 50 per cent to a record high in January 2021. Most of those gains were lost in the next two years as the Reserve Bank started to hike interest rates. Much the same thing happened to the property market, with house prices tracking the same path as shares: up sharply as interest rates were slashed, and then down sharply as rate hikes began.

The pandemic bubble was an exaggerated version of something we'd been grappling with since central banks first slashed interest rates during the GFC. Low rates through the 2010s saw equity and property markets boom. In fact, with inflation under control from the mid-1990s, you can make the case that both property and equity markets sailed along on the fair winds for almost 30 years. Sounds great — right?

But there's also a strong case to be made that low rates and low inflation drove the huge lift in social inequality we saw through that period. Essentially, the economy made it easy for those with assets to create more wealth, while those relying on wage growth struggled.

Low interest rates are good for stability and good markets because they encourage borrowing and investment by companies, which drives productivity and growth. But if they are too low, that is really just a symptom of a deflationary economy where confidence in the future is low. Like everything in economics, finding the right setting is a trade-off. Broadly speaking, we know that it is bad news if prices are rising too fast and bad news if they are not rising at all. But finding the sweet spot and holding the economy there is not easy.

The history of modern economies is a story of central banks gaining and losing control of inflation. Graphs showing inflation levels and interest rates settings across time are like fossil records of our economic fortunes.

Chapter 11

The hard sell: Monopolies and marketing

Advertising is legalised lying.
— H. G. Wells

....

There is another crucial layer of influence on price. The price we pay for things is determined by businesspeople seeking to maximise profit from what they do. Their efforts might trigger inflation or add to it. But they are independent of the big inflationary flow of money supply; this is about individual actors doing what they can to get the best price. One of the most obvious ways to ensure you get the best price is to create monopolies on supply. Less competition means more freedom to demand a higher price.

When people start a business, they tend to think about coming up with something new that people can't get anywhere else. When new technologies emerge, the inventors often have a monopoly — at least for a while.

But monopolies, where one supplier has complete dominance of a market, distort supply and demand curves by vesting too much power to the supply side. Monopolies are generally seen as bad for society. They are inefficient, as there's little pressure to keep costs under control and prices down. They also hurt economies by limiting competition, which means the dominant business has less incentive to invest in improving things, and innovation is stifled.

That's why competition laws are one area where even the most hardened free-market libertarians can see there is a place for some government regulation. The issues those folks have with inefficient governments are much the same as the issues around private monopolies. Without competition, even the best of us can get lazy.

So, most modern economies have rules in place, and enforcement agencies with the power to break up companies if they become too dominant. More competition is generally seen as a good way to drive prices down and stimulate innovation.

The lack of competition in the New Zealand economy is a constant frustration for those concerned that the cost of living is too high here. Unlike bigger markets in Australia or the US and UK, our small population makes it harder for multiple players to remain viable in any given industry. We often struggle to sustain more than three. We have a Commerce Commission that does its best to ensure we have at least two operators in most sectors.

For example, when it comes to supermarkets, we talk a lot about a duopoly. There are several supermarket brands, but most are owned by two big companies: Foodstuffs and Woolworths. Other industries where competition is light in New Zealand, and regulation is needed, include the banks, petrol companies, airlines, major liquor companies, telecommunication companies and even power companies (on a regional basis).

With the government under pressure on inflation and the cost of living, we have seen increasing regulatory attention fall on industries that look like they lack competition. Banks, supermarkets and petrol companies have all been subject to pricing studies. But beyond sending them a stern letter of warning, what can governments really do?

Actually, if they really want to, governments can legislate to limit the size of companies and force them to sell down their assets. The government did that to Telecom in 2006, forcing it to sell off its lines business (which became Chorus) to create more competition in the market. It worked, though it was controversial, costing investors a lot of money and earning the Labour government of the day plenty of pushback.

Many people still believe that the dominance of two or three big players in most sectors is one of the reasons Kiwis pay more for consumer goods and services than overseas peers. But their arguments run up against an underlying fear that having too many operators in such a small market isn't commercially viable.

Since the Telecom split, neither of the two major political parties has shown any appetite for legislating to break up big players in other industries. In fact, the Commerce Commission controversially allowed some very big industry mergers in the 2000s. For example, Woolworths was allowed to buy supermarket rival Progressive Enterprises in 2005, effectively creating a duopoly in the industry. And in 2003, Australian bank ANZ was allowed an exemption to the Commerce Act to buy rival National Bank.

I'll come back to this country's troubled relationship with banking when I look at the housing market.

Rise of the Mad Men

When companies don't have monopolies, they have to compete for your attention. They need to convince you that their version of a product is best. This seems a healthier state of affairs. Marketing and advertising are the dark arts that capitalism brings to bear on the price of things. But at least they are evidence of companies making an effort. There are rules and regulations about how companies are allowed to advertise that stuff, too, but they are generally a lot more permissive than competition law.

For a small country, New Zealand has a good track record for creating popular local brands with peculiar Kiwi characteristics. There's a lot of mythologising around stereotypes of rugged individualism, farmers and bushmen of the kind that once dominated local movies and novels.

There's the advertising for Speight's beer, where southern men on horses laugh about soft Aucklanders, or Mainland Cheese where old men sit around country cheese factories competing for the most laconic sense of humour. More latterly, Kiwi brands have tried to tap into New Zealand's progressive 'clean, green' image — none more successfully, perhaps, than our own Tourism Board's '100% Pure' marketing campaign. Of course, whether we are still 100 per cent pure is questionable – just try swimming in a river – but marketing has always taken a bit of creative licence.

The practice has ancient roots. There are examples of brands of fish sauce being advertised in ancient Rome, with tile mosaics touting quality and price. Modern consumer brands and adverts became common throughout the nineteenth century as billboards and printed publications like newspapers took off. But it was the mass production and mass communication of the twentieth century that really put advertising on steroids.

The ad men co-opted pop music, and the advertising world planted jingles in our brains that would stay with us for life – all in the name of creating brands that enable the extraction of higher prices. Most New Zealanders of a certain age could still sing a few lines from the Ches and Dale cheese ads or the Crunchie bar train robbery song. In the era with just two TV channels, we all watched the same things and advertising became a point of shared cultural identity.

If advertising was powerful stuff back then, the rise of the internet has injected it with even stronger fuel. Now we're living with a wild-eyed, angry marketing monster, hopped up on steroids and punching its way directly into our serotonin receptors, or whatever part of the brain controls our deepest desires.

If the internet catches me looking at sneakers, some artificially intelligent marketing algorithm rats me out, and suddenly I get sneaker ads in my social media feed for days.

The trouble is, I really like sneakers. I keep scrolling through them. I don't need them, but I desire them. And of course, desire has always been a powerful driver of demand, especially in a world where our basic needs are met. In fact, price seems to be greatly influenced by all our human frailties.

Advertisers know this all too well. The seven deadly sins – pride, greed, wrath, envy, lust, gluttony and sloth – are all solid sales drivers. (The Bible also had seven heavenly virtues: prudence, justice, temperance, fortitude, faith, hope and charity. I don't think any of those sell a lot of sneakers.)

Selling identity

Clever brand marketing has tapped into our psychological need to feel part of a community. Brands present themselves as unique subcultures which can give us a sense of identity and belonging. And of course, the privilege of belonging comes at a price.

Business has made a science of understanding this desire. Back in the 1930s, marketing was established as an academic discipline by a professor and economist from the University of Illinois called Paul D. Converse, who sadly has nothing to do with the sneakers of the same name. He described marketing as a combination of psychology, economics, management science and accounting.

Over the years the industry has become clinical in its ability to, not just sell us stuff, but to tell us stories about that stuff to make it seem special, to add a premium and drive up the price. Why should one kind of sneaker be three times the price of another? It's all just marketing hype, right? It's not real. Good luck arguing that case at the mall, with a teenager comparing a pair of Air Jordans with a pair of non-brand sneakers.

I'm old enough to remember when adidas and Nike first arrived in New Zealand and wiped homegrown Bata Bullets and Skellerup All Stars from the sports fields of the nation. Yes, this is another sneaker analogy, but it illustrates another obsession: New Zealand's radical transformation to an open-market economy in the early 1980s.

You could make the case that the arrival of all those foreign sneakers was a brutal corporate colonisation of the nation's sportswear. But New Zealand's folksy homespun advertising, as catchy as it was, couldn't compete with the deeper emotional connections that international brands were dreaming up. Let's face it, the Americans and Germans also made comfier, more elegant sneakers, with much more compelling marketing stories behind them. We didn't care about the price; we paid it.

Chapter 12

How commodities hit your pocket

For what were all these country patriots born?
To hunt, and vote, and raise the price of corn?
— Byron, 'The Age of Bronze'

....

L et's forget about the corporates and their slick marketing departments for a while and get back to our basic needs: food, energy ... and coffee.

The most basic of commodities are traded on complex markets that influence what we pay for products at the supermarket and, sometimes, the fortunes of whole economies. Food, for example, is not a want. It's a need. Feeding yourself is one of the primary animal behaviours (the capuchin monkeys highlighted the other one).

But of course, when it comes to food, there's eating to sustain and there's eating to indulge. There's a bowl of rice, and there's a wagyu steak with shaved truffle and gold leaf flakes. Once we get past the subsistence value of food, it quickly falls prey to all those other decadent influences. Between the farm and your plate, the processing of foodstuffs into ever more delicious variations shifts food away from being a basic commodity, all the while adding value.

You'll often hear terms like 'value-add' in discussion about the New Zealand economy. As a nation we are very good at producing and shipping commodities. But for decades we've been trying to work out how to move beyond selling animal carcasses and dehydrated milk to the world, and despite considerable effort and a few great success stories, we've never quite managed it.

Companies like Kiwi dairy giant Fonterra have invested heavily in marketing and brands, but have never managed to emulate food manufacturers such as Switzerland's Nestlé or America's Kraft. So New Zealand's economy remains highly influenced by the rises and falls of commodity markets. We've looked for ways to add value by turning milk into yoghurt, butter or cheese and creating our own brands. We've done okay at that, but not great. Fonterra's Anchor brand — founded way back in 1886 — is a success story, with 160 products sold into 80 countries. But it has still struggled for market dominance against the branding might of Nestlé and Kraft.

Other value-added pathways include the mining of milk powder for more complex protein ingredients that can be used in enriched foods and sports drinks.

New Zealand famously missed a huge opportunity to cash in on one of its biggest-ever marketing success stories: the global reinvention of a fruit we almost (allegedly) called the hairyberry.

The kiwifruit's original name, Chinese gooseberry, reflected its country of origin and its small size. But it grew well in the New Zealand climate, and some successful selective breeding created a much larger fruit. From the first plantings in 1905, it became a distinctly Kiwi fruit. It proved popular with visiting US and Australian servicemen during the Second World War, and exports kicked off in the early 1950s. 'Hairyberry' was never going to get that funny oval-shaped thing onto the plates of California billionaires or Japanese businessmen. Instead, the kiwifruit was christened in 1959 by Jack Turner from Turners & Growers to promote marketing campaigns in the US.

With the possible exception of the national rugby team, the kiwifruit has been New Zealand's greatest marketing success. We took a fruit that had previously been an exotic oddity and catapulted it into the big league of apples and bananas. But we failed to take ownership of the trademark (which was never registered internationally) and licensing rights around its name and so missed the opportunity to create a valuable commercial brand.

Thankfully, better late than never, the industry created its own brand in 1997.

Zespri and the cooperative export company that it represents have done well since and added value with popular new varieties like Kiwi Gold.

The rise in demand for healthy, organic produce has changed the game in the last couple of decades. For some farmers, adding value comes from working out how to improve the care of animals, or producing foods without recourse to chemical pesticides.

That's when marketing departments get involved. The way we sell our beef is a good case in point. We often look across the Tasman and bemoan our lack of natural resources such as oil, gas and iron ore. But one of New Zealand's great natural advantages has always been its ability to grow grass. It rains a lot here, and we have good soil.

Our sheep and cattle herds have been grass-fed and free-range since the beginning of farming here — not because foreign markets liked the welfare aspects, but because it was cheap and easy. For many years, this was a downside from a sales point of view. Northern hemisphere consumers did not like the taste of grass-fed beef or dairy, finding it too strong compared to the grain-fed, factory-farmed meat they were used to. It's only recently that 'grass-fed' has become a valuable marketing term as American and European consumers have embraced it as a kinder, more environmentally sound way of farming.

We've made some progress adding brand value to our commodities by marketing the whole country as a clean, green place. Overall, though, New Zealand has done well as a commodity producer because it wins on cost. That's because for a long time New Zealand also had cheap power, thanks to the big hydroelectric projects, so we had a competitive advantage when it came to turning large quantities of milk into powder. We were able to dominate the global powdered milk market.

By the turn of the millennium, though, after a decade of falling global commodity prices, this reliance on the low-cost model was seen as a dead-end strategy. Luckily, the historic rise of the Chinese consumer in the twenty-first century has boosted demand for protein-rich food and kept the commodity business very lucrative. That said, the return of strong commodity prices is a double-edged sword.

New Zealand has certainly benefited economically, but the downside is that it distracted us from efforts to add value to our products and escape our dependence on fickle commodity markets. Now, as China's economy slows (with some fearing a Japanese-style demographic shift), we find ourselves again facing over-reliance on a single market and at the mercy of global commodity trends.

The global trade lottery

Wheat, rice, seed and oils, meat and dairy: all the basic foodstuffs are traded on global markets which set a price that flows through every part of the economy. When commodity prices rise, it's good news for food-producing countries like New Zealand, since higher prices mean more export dollars flowing into the economy.

But there are downsides. One is the lack of control we have over price. Fonterra is big enough that it has some influence on commodity prices owing to the sheer volume of dairy product it can put into the global market. It is the world's largest single exporter of dairy product, accounting for about 30 per cent of global product (bearing in mind that the big European and US companies primarily supply their massive domestic markets). If New Zealand farmers have a dry summer and production is down, this can cause a global supply shortage, and prices rise. It's a good natural hedge for our farmers.

Fonterra can't control commodity prices with anything like the power that consumer goods companies like Nestlé can with their value-added, shopper-ready brands. That leaves Fonterra and its farmers — and the New Zealand economy by proxy — at the mercy of global price trends, which move on major weather events or the economic fortunes of important markets like China. Despite efforts to diversify our economy away from meat and dairy commodities, Fonterra still accounts for something like 20 per cent of all New Zealand's export earnings, and China now accounts for around 30 per cent of all our exports.

GLOBAL DAIRY EXPORTS (2022)

(Source: https://www.worldstopexports.com/top-milk-exporting-countries/)

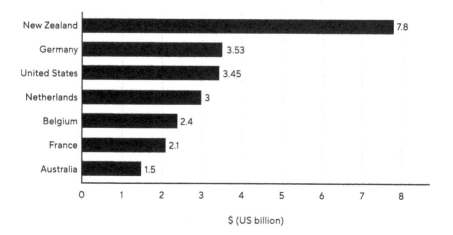

$ (US billion)

High dairy prices are good for New Zealand on balance because they bring in more foreign currency, growing the economy. But because the global market sets the price for *all* dairy ingredients, New Zealand consumers, too, feel the price rises, and that's how we end up paying more for cheese at the supermarket (which can seem unfair, given how much of it we produce). So, if New Zealand food exporters are too successful in extracting high global prices, then locals may not be able to afford the homegrown produce.

Sadly, this also happens in a lot of developing countries. Some of the biggest producers of cocoa in the world — like the Ivory Coast and Cameroon — are among the poorest nations in the world. That means that consumers there can't afford to eat a lot of the chocolate their crops produce. In fact, it happens in New Zealand, too, with high-end seafoods, like scampi, which seldom even make it to local restaurants, let alone supermarkets, because the price they command internationally is so high.

Expensive scampi we can cope with. But, as people found out when inflation spiked after the pandemic, the price of more basic foodstuffs is fundamental to our well-being. At the most brutal level, we see what happens when production and distribution of food break down completely due to war, drought and corruption. People starve. In a world where we have the scientific ability to produce food in abundance, it is shocking that this is still happening.

The political revolutions of the Arab Spring in 2010 had their roots in the social unrest sparked by rising food prices after the GFC. The hike in food prices came as economies bounced back after the financial crisis while production was not yet back in full swing. The world was also getting to grips with the surge in consumer demand from China, where the economy was growing by more than 10 per cent a year. In Tunisia and Egypt in 2010 it was bread prices that sparked riots which ended in political revolution.

Around the world, an intense focus on one culturally important product is often seen when a country's prices spike. In Indonesia it's chillies, and in India it's onions; in China there has been social unrest over the price of pork and rice. Food-price inflation at that time caused a stir in New Zealand, too, and our triggering product is − you guessed it − cheese.

Whenever commodity prices rise, you can be sure that media stories about the excessive price of cheese are not far away. No amount of chin-stroking *Business Herald* articles about the upside for New Zealand's current account can stop the panic when cheese prices rise. The idea of eating less than a kilogram of cheese a week is culturally unthinkable to many Kiwis, so I just roll with it now.

Seriously, though, food price rises do hit the poor hardest, because the grocery bill is usually one of the biggest fixed costs we face. This oversized impact on poorer people is true of all inflation. They typically have to spend a greater proportion of their total income to get by, which means they feel rising prices more acutely. We have seen it all again in the past few years. Grain prices spiked after the Russian invasion of Ukraine in 2021, delivering an extra shot of global inflationary pressure at a time when it was already becoming a problem.

Commodity food ingredients like wheat, milk powder and sugar are omnipresent in our processed foods. They are the high-energy fuels on which Western civilisation has been built. Unlike fruit and vegetables, they are heavily traded commodities. That means the 'real world' effects of supply shortfalls caused by weather (or war) are exaggerated by traders, who start buying up futures from the moment they hear storm clouds are starting to form.

Commodities have derivative markets which trade set prices for future delivery. They were designed to provide price certainty for farmers and let them hedge against seasonal fluctuations (see 'A derivative diversion', page 208). But they can fall prey to speculative investors looking to make quick returns on price fluctuations. That can add an extra frustrating dimension to supermarket prices.

It takes time – usually around six to nine months – for big commodity price spikes to flow through to consumers, though, which is why local consumers often don't get really upset about the price of cheese until well after the dairy boom has peaked. It can make for confusing overlaps in news coverage, with stories about export prices often at odds with stories about shopping bills.

Food prices are a serious business. We need to treat access to food not as an investment category but as a human right, not least because lack of access can lead to social breakdown. At a press conference back in 2008, then US Federal Reserve chairman Ben Bernanke was forced to deny that the stimulatory US monetary policy was causing inflation and exacerbating the food spike. 'It's entirely unfair to attribute excess demand issues in emerging markets to US monetary policy,' the UK *Daily Telegraph* quoted him saying. 'Excess demand issues – well, that's one way of talking about hungry people,' a reader comment on the news website observed.

That line stuck with me.

PRICE OF YOUR TAKEAWAY COFFEE*

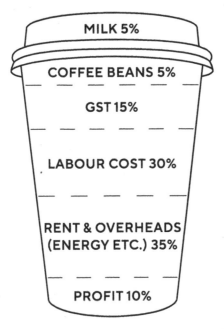

MILK 5%

COFFEE BEANS 5%

GST 15%

LABOUR COST 30%

RENT & OVERHEADS (ENERGY ETC.) 35%

PROFIT 10%

*Author's estimate based on local and international media stories (exact ratios will vary for individual businesses).

Conspiracies, supply chains and your daily flat white

For a lot of the things we buy, the price of the raw ingredient — the commodity — is just a small component of what we end up paying. The more steps involved in bringing a product to us, the more complicated its pricing. Inflation in its purest sense — as a by-product of excess money supply — plays a role all the way through the supply chain process, because it lifts costs every step of the way. More expensive energy and labour add to what we pay and weaken the direct correlation between commodity prices and the price of the end product.

Consider the price of a takeaway coffee. Stories warning that it's about to get more expensive are perennial media favourites. Typically, a headline will warn that the price is going to rise based on some distant news about weather events or political disruption in Brazil. Business writers jump at the chance to publish a popular story, making commodity price news relatable by equating it to the price of our daily flat white.

But big spikes (or slumps) in raw coffee bean prices seldom end up flowing through to us to any meaningful extent. That's because the price of a barista-made coffee includes rent, labour costs, milk, expensive machinery, a cup, and all the rest of the daily business costs, like the power needed to heat the water.Cafés do put prices up when they face rising costs, but they are limited in their capacity to do that by the level of elasticity in demand for coffee.

Even though caffeine is a mildly addictive drug, if the price of a café flat white rises too far, then people may decide they are okay with making one at home. Or switching to tea.

CHEESE ON TOAST: THE POWER OF PRICE ELASTICITY

How much would the price of a takeaway coffee have to rise before you gave up and made it at home? Or, as an economist would put it, how elastic is the price of that coffee?

Price elasticity is simply a term that refers to how much demand for a product will rise or fall depending on rises or falls in price. There are exceptions but, as a general rule, products that are discretionary in our lives tend to be inelastic, because we can easily substitute them with something else if the price rises too high. Seasonal vegetables are a good example. When avocados are cheap and in season, we might eat them every day. But as the price rises, demand drops off because they are nice to have but not an essential food.

Products that people are less able to go without tend to be quite elastic. Meth dealers presumably enjoy the benefits of elastic pricing. Once people are hooked, they lose a lot of discretion around what they are prepared to pay for their hit.

Tobacco, petrol and booze fall into this category. All of these are subject to government taxes that are designed to discourage demand. So, as well as the companies that produce those products being worried about how much they can charge before demand falls, governments are interested in the extent to which extra tax diminishes demand.

In the end almost everything has a point at which demand will fall. Research suggests some (although sadly not all) smokers will quit as the price rises. Oil producers like OPEC have always had to be careful about pushing prices too high as people do start to drive less, or ride a bike or take public transport. These days we can also choose to drive electric cars.

Economists use a simple equation to get a rough guide to the elasticity of a product. The percentage change in quantity demanded is divided by the percentage change in price. That generates a number greater than or smaller than one (or exactly one if demand and price are exactly in sync). If the number is greater than one, then the product is elastic. In other words, consumers are highly responsive to price changes, and small price increases will cause larger decreases in the quantity demanded, and vice versa. If the number is less than one, it is inelastic: the percentage change in quantity demanded is less than the percentage change in price. In other words, consumers aren't greatly influenced by price changes, and even significant price increases result in only minor decreases in demand.

Businesses usually like to make their products as inelastic as possible. As well as selling products we are addicted to, they can do that by having a monopoly on a market. That makes price elasticity an important tool for regulators seeking to ensure markets are competitive. The cleverest companies do it by creating brands with powerful emotional connections to consumers. Because if we love a brand, we're inclined to stick with it, even if the price rises.

Price elasticity will also vary in different markets for a variety of cultural and socio-economic reasons. New Zealand dairy exporters, for example, worry about the elasticity of products like cheese in relatively new markets like China. When the price of dairy rises too high, demand for products like pizza can fall because that kind of food is relatively new in China. In New Zealand, where that 1 kilogram block of cheese is almost a staple food, the price is far more inelastic. We might complain about the price, but we are not going without our cheese on toast.

This is the point in any 'flat white' analysis of economics where I expect to hear the espresso drinkers pipe up and complain about paying too much for their short black. It's a fair point. An espresso requires no milk, and much less hot water, and is much quicker and easier to make — so theoretically requires less labour. Its price probably should correlate more directly with the commodity price of coffee beans. But the business administration work involved in adjusting the price more frequently than a flat white makes the idea ridiculous. Maybe, if café owners could be bothered, the price of an espresso could change daily.

Weirdly, that happens with another consumer product we buy regularly. Petrol prices go up and down rapidly, based on commodity market moves, even though this product also involves a great deal of processing and transporting, in this case to get from the ground to your car.

Unfortunately for the planet, oil is still a special product. The global economy runs on the stuff. It's not just the cost of filling up the car that creates inflation when oil prices rise. Almost everyone is using petrol to transport everything else we buy and consume. Oil is used to make plastics, so it influences the price of manufacturing and packaging. So, despite our desire to be less reliant on the stuff, oil price stability is still fundamental to the price of everything.

Because of that, the price of oil makes a great barometer for the overall state of the global economy. It provides an instant snapshot of global demand, like a scoreboard for the epic battle between inflationary and deflationary trends. If the oil price is soaring, then we are dealing with a hot economy and risk of inflation taking hold. If it slumps, then we could be looking at recession and dangerous price deflation.

The forces shifting the oil price are complex. There's Middle Eastern politics, for starters. It just so happens that much of the world's most easily accessible oil reserves are in Arab nations, where unrest in various manifestations has had a direct effect on global economies. The US has also put itself in the thick of it all — not least because its economy is so reliant on cheap oil — which has had huge political ramifications.

The first truly world-shaking oil price spike was in 1973, when OPEC first got its act together with efforts to control the price: it imposed an embargo on the US and other countries that had supported Israel in the Yom Kippur War, and the price of oil soared by 300 per cent. There was a second oil shock in 1979 when Iran and Iraq went to war and oil production slumped. These price shocks coincided with the expansionary postwar Keynesian economic policies the West was running at the time. They played a big part in that horrible 20 years of high inflation that I keep going on about.

In New Zealand the oil shocks also coincided with a big fall in our export earnings as the UK joined Europe and our agricultural products faced tariffs and quotas. So, while the price of oil was just one factor, you could make the case that it played a key role in the late-1970s economic meltdown and all those years of political turmoil and reform that followed.

Since those two big shocks, though, OPEC has never really been able to control pricing as much as it would like. OPEC members include most of the big Middle Eastern oil producers — Iran, Iraq, Kuwait, Saudi Arabia and the United Arab Emirates — as well as Venezuela and some of the African producers, such as Nigeria and Libya. They still meet regularly and try to agree on production targets to optimise the price for their members. One issue they face now is that the US has massively increased its domestic production of oil and is less reliant on OPEC's supply. The other issue is one that provides another great example of how silly most conspiracy theories are.

Conspiracy theorists love wild theories that the world is secretly controlled by an elite cabal of billionaires who pull the strings of the deep state. When it comes to oil, there is nothing secret about it. There literally is a small group of people who get together in a room and try to control the price of the oil. But humans are bad at agreeing on anything for any length of time. So, since the 1970s, all the big oil shocks have been slumps: sudden plunges in the price of oil that threw markets into turmoil. More often than not, OPEC members fail to agree on production targets and accidentally oversupply the market.

For most of the years I've been writing about oil, the biggest concern has been too much oil on the market. For a while after those 1970s shocks, it was assumed that oil was going to become increasingly scarce. But technology has put paid to those fears, and the controversial technique of fracking – blasting water, sand and chemicals into shale rock to flush oil out of the cracks – has enabled the US to more than double its production in the past decade. Fracking is not as cost-efficient as pumping oil straight out of the ground. But now, if OPEC does try to limit production and pushes the price too high, then US shale oil production becomes profitable and ramps up.

The price of petrol – taxes aside – has continued to fall as producers apply new technology to extract previously marginal oil deposits. Relatively speaking, running a gas-guzzler in 2019 is much cheaper than it was in the 1980s.

One recent exception to that trend was the big price spike after Russia invaded Ukraine in early 2022. A Western embargo on Russian oil created an immediate supply shortage at a time when US production had fallen away because of the pandemic lockdowns reducing demand. As with food, the shock came at a bad time for the global economy. But the high prices didn't last. The US ramped up production, and prices fell back to pre-war levels within a year.

Since then, we've seen the Saudis working with the Russians to make production cuts independently of OPEC and push up oil prices. Some Western commentators have interpreted that as a partially political move, designed to undermine US and European efforts to beat inflation. But US shale oil effectively puts a cap on the global oil price — which is not necessarily a good thing when you consider the ecological impacts of burning fossil fuels.

It's likely oil prices will fall even further in coming years as petrol-driven cars compete with increasingly cost-efficient electric alternatives. The 2022 price shock was a reminder that we are still dependent on oil, but at least demand is finally showing signs of elasticity because viable substitutes are gradually coming onto the market.

Ultimately, oil makes hypocrites of us all. We desperately want to stop using it to save the planet. We should all be cheering on ever higher prices, hoping that crude oil runs out sooner rather than later. But because oil prices remain one of the biggest single drivers of price in the world, we don't do that. When we get a shock, like we did in 2022, we all squeal about higher prices at the petrol pump. Government cuts fuel taxes, the US ups its fracking, and we all pray that OPEC will all agree to up its supply.

Here's hoping technology wins the race and, someday soon, short-term price shocks elicit no more than a shrug of our collective shoulders.

You set the price

All these big economic forces are well beyond our individual control. In a small country like New Zealand even the government has very little control over them. But for most of us, at least those of us not on the breadline, there is still plenty of personal discretion in how we view price.

Think about the most expensive thing you ever bought. I don't mean your house. That's inevitably got the biggest number attached, and you have to live somewhere. (I'll dive deep into that one in the next chapter.) I mean the most indulgent, over-the-top purchase you ever made.

For me it's probably a designer suede leather jacket for which I forked out about $500 in 1990. I'd struggle to spend $500 on any one item of clothing these days, but the grungy brown Ermenegildo Zegna jacket I forked out for as an 18-year-old probably cost about $3000 in today's inflation-adjusted dollars. I was technically a poor student at the time, but I must have been feeling flush with my new part-time job. Or it went on the student loan, I can't really remember. Anyway, I had to have that jacket, even though it was almost the same as the kind of brown suede jackets you found in op shops at the time for $50.

The jacket was a huge success. A girl I had fancied at high school, but who had climbed the university social ladder far higher than I, told me it was cool. Within a year, grunge rock had broken big and a similar brown suede jacket worn by Pearl Jam's Eddie Vedder had seriously diminished my jacket's cool factor. Whatever. I still love the memory of that jacket.

I suspect that a lot of our most indulgent purchases are items of clothing we paid well over the odds for. Or it's the flash gear we splashed out on to add enjoyment to a hobby — surfboards, mountain bikes or even fancy cars. Or experiences, a holiday or a gourmet meal we couldn't really afford. Supply and demand tell us how price is determined by what someone is prepared to pay for something. But that's quite abstract until it's you who is staring at the price. What something is worth to you is what matters, and that can be a complex equation full of personal bias.

Humans are a strange bunch, and we complicate economics with our weird psychology.

Chapter 13

Safe as houses: Why Kiwis are obsessed with property prices

You can't live in a stock certificate.
— Oprah Winfrey

....

Welcome to the inevitable gruelling, divisive discussion about New Zealand house prices. If you've read a few of my think-pieces about housing, you'll know this is the chapter where I berate Kiwis for investing in property instead of tracking the stock market with a balanced investment portfolio. Or something like that.

Perhaps I could go with one of those reactionary rants instead. I could moan about how young people have only themselves to blame for being perpetual renters. 'It wasn't easy in my day, either, and we didn't have spare money for flat whites and avocado toast, you know. You have to make sacrifices.'

Okay, boomer. Actually, I'm Generation X. I'm pretty sure we did have money for flat whites and avocado toast, and we bought houses, too (although it might have been cappuccinos and Eggs Benedict back in the 1990s). Of course, a café brunch was much cheaper then — like the houses!

We've already covered New Zealand's economic history, but I need to recap a bit here, because it can all look a bit different when viewed through the lens of the housing market.

New Zealanders have always loved property. We were once the land of the quarter-acre paradise. A crisp, neatly mown lawn out the front, a vegetable garden out the back and a tidy, if somewhat draughty, weatherboard home. My grandparents Harry and Phyllis Inwood got theirs with a returned serviceman's loan after World War Two. It *was* a kind of paradise for men like Harry. The war had turned his world upside down and robbed him of his youth, and after settling on his patch of land in south Christchurch he had no ambition ever to move again.

Having lived through the Great Depression and the war, many New Zealanders similarly embraced the quiet suburban life in the 1950s and 1960s. And mostly they could afford it, even if they were working class (as my grandparents were) and didn't have much cash. The population was small, land was plentiful, and the economy was buoyant. Obviously, there was poverty and social dysfunction, but by and large it was 'out of sight and out of mind' for urban Pākehā.

As we saw earlier, governments on both the left and right were following the hands-on Keynesian postwar economic policies of the US and UK, providing more social support than there had ever been before. Our economy boomed off the back of demand for food exports as the UK went into postwar reconstruction mode, and New Zealand finally had the wealth it needed to realise the 'cradle to grave' welfare state envisioned by Prime Minister Michael Joseph Savage in the 1930s.

Of course, those conditions didn't last. When the UK joined the European Economic Community in 1973, export earnings dwindled, and we were on a collision course for the big free-market social upheaval. But even the turmoil of the late 1970s–80s didn't cause New Zealand's housing market to soar dramatically or to crash.

From the mid-1970s to about 1983, house prices declined significantly as we suffered a brain drain and net migration outflow. When prices took off again after 1984 there were extremely high interest rates to deal with. It was a time of high inflation, but wages grew along with prices, keeping some sense of affordability in the market.

My parents bought a run-down bungalow in Beckenham, Christchurch, for $9000 in 1974. Six years later, they traded up to a house with a view in lower Cashmere for $36,000. Dad was a senior teacher and Mum had a part-time job at the Canterbury Savings Bank, back then part of a network of 14 community-owned provincial banks. Paying the mortgage was a stretch when the interest rates spiked in the mid-1980s, up to an eye-watering 20 per cent in 1987.

I've interviewed many New Zealanders about life in this era and there are many similar stories. People talk about how tough it was for families to get by week to week as living costs spiralled. I recall how broke my parents were through the mid-1980s trying to service the mortgage and deal with the demands of three kids in an increasingly consumerist world. An open economy meant the sudden arrival of cool international stuff in New Zealand. We 'needed' Cabbage Patch Kids, adidas sneakers, Casio Space Invaders calculators and Soda Streams (we got the cheaper, lesser-known Merry Mix soft drink system). There certainly wasn't a lot of spare money. For a while our family didn't pass what would become John Key's simple and popular definition of wealth: not having to worry if the washing machine or car broke down. Mum's wages helped; her staff-discounted mortgage rate was probably a saviour. But there weren't any café brunches for Mum and Dad (not that Christchurch offered many options for that in the 1980s), and even eating dinner out was a rare treat involving Cobb & Co. or the Oxford Pub & Restaurant.

My point is that most Kiwis did not have much spare cash, and by many measures the economy was in the worst shape it had been in since the Great Depression. Apart, that is, from one small detail: the housing market was generally a lot, lot cheaper. Although New Zealanders didn't have the equity or purchasing power that many do now, we were a more equal society.

MEASURING INEQUALITY

When we think about a more equal society, we generally think in aspirational terms about a better and wealthier world. But of course, there are plenty of examples of societies being equal in their misery.

While the roots of poverty in many nations have plenty to do with colonisation and exploitation, there are also examples of efforts to enforce or engineer equality that effectively just drag down the whole economy. Countries throughout Asia, South America, Africa and Eastern Europe can offer many examples, sadly.

Economists sometimes use a scale called the Gini coefficient to quantify and illustrate inequality in a society. Devised by Italian sociologist Corrado Gini, the OECD describes it as a 'comparison of cumulative proportions of the population against cumulative proportions of income they receive'.[10] It indexes countries with a number (or fraction of a number) in the case of perfect equality, and one in the case of perfect inequality. Sometimes this can be multiplied by 100 and presented as a percentage for easier interpretation, with 0 per cent representing perfect equality and 100 per cent perfect inequality.

When you look at the ranking of all the world's countries based on their Gini coefficient it is easy to see that the most politically and economically troubled countries generally have a high number and are most unequal. South Africa tops the World Bank's list. New Zealand, Germany, the UK and the US sit somewhere in the middle, albeit with varying degrees of inequality.[11]

But it's not a straightforward equation in which more equality equals more wealth. The US rates a 41.5 — not too far off the Democratic Republic of the Congo at 42.1. Some of the most equal countries aren't that wealthy — former communist states like the Slovak Republic and Belarus, for example.

New Zealand was famously egalitarian from the days of the First Labour Government, which launched the welfare

10   'Income Inequality', OECD, https://data.oecd.org/inequality/income-inequality.htm.

11   'Gini Index', World Bank, https://data.worldbank.org/indicator/SI.POV.GINI?most_recent_value_desc=true.

state with the Social Security Act 1938. Even on through the craziness of the 1980s, things were relatively stable. According to the Ministry of Economic Development this country had a Gini coefficient of 27 in 1983.[12] But the latest OECD figure is 36.2 — a big rise. It seems we are becoming a less equitable nation. Sadly, it seems safe to assume, that slide is tied up with the brutal divide that our housing boom has opened.

Something changed in the 1990s, and house prices took off. For years, what we had was an ideal market environment for handy Kiwis to make a few dollars renovating old villas and selling them on — and that kind of became part of our culture. Yes, there were market cycles — but they were slow and shallow, playing out over years. But then the market got crazy: data shows that prices began accelerating in the mid-1990s,[13] and it's got crazier and crazier since then.

What changed?

LONG-TERM HOUSE PRICES

(Source: https://www.globalpropertyguide.com/pacific/new-zealand/home-price-trends)

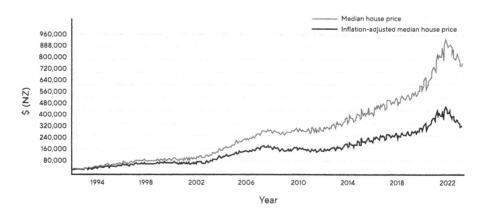

12   'The Social Report 2016 — Te pūrongo oranga tangata', Ministry of Social Development Te Manatū Whakahiato Ora, https://socialreport.msd.govt.nz/economic-standard-of-living/income-inequality.html.

13   'New Zealand Housing Index', Trading Economics, https://tradingeconomics.com/new-zealand/housing-index.

We have lift-off

By the mid-1990s we had more or less beaten inflation; interest rates were coming back down to earth, so borrowing was becoming cheaper again. It was also getting easier. Lower interest rates alone might have just taken us back to the market dynamic of the 1950s and 1960s — but after the wild ride of 1970s inflation and 1980s free-market reform, we made a political decision to open our banking system to foreign capital. Actually, that is just a fancy way of saying we sold all our banks.

The arguments made at the time for these sales were that international ownership would bring more investment, more efficiency and more competition to the market. Up until the late 1980s, the state owned four major banks: PostBank (Post Office Savings Bank), the Bank of New Zealand, Rural Bank and the Development Finance Corporation (for business lending). There was also the regional network of provincial community-owned Trust Banks and the British-owned National Bank. Building societies and other non-bank finance companies were also active and significant players in the lending market, making up 20 per cent of the sector by 1984. So New Zealanders did have a choice in the old days, but the sector lacked access to international capital, so lenders were conservative and getting a mortgage was extremely tough.

With the arrival of the new Labour government in 1984, we opened our markets to the world, then over the next two decades we sold off all our banks. In 1989, ANZ bought PostBank from the government for $665 million. The Commonwealth Bank of Australia bought 75 per cent of the ASB Bank in 1989 (it got the rest in 2000). BNZ almost collapsed. It was bailed out by the government in 1990 and then sold to the National Australia Bank in 1992 for $1.5 billion. Around the same time, nine regional savings banks merged into Trust Bank, and then in 1996 they sold out to Sydney-based Westpac for $1.2 billion. Countrywide took over the former United Building Society and then sold the combined business to the National Bank. The National Bank also bought the Rural Bank.

So, by 2001, we had five big banks all owned in Australia or Britain, and controlling 90 per cent of the country's bank assets. In 2003 we actually bent the rules of the Commerce Act to allow ANZ to buy National, consolidating the sector even further with the Aussies.

One of the reasons we sold them — perhaps foolishly, and certainly too cheaply — was that we wanted international banks with access to more capital to get the economy humming. I think, if we're honest, the asset sales were also driven by a desperation for money (the Crown accounts were in dire shape), and we had a dismal lack of confidence in our own ability to do things like telecommunications and finance and banking.

Whatever you think of the sale process, it did create an environment of much easier lending conditions. Unfortunately, the capital didn't all flow to productive new businesses or technology start-ups, or whatever else we hoped would transform the economy back then. Instead, it mostly flowed into housing. We gave our gentle 'do up and sell' property culture a powerful boost. Actually, it was more of an *Incredible Hulk*-level radioactive steroid shot.

Since the mid-1990s, the average price of a Kiwi house has increased by more than 600 per cent. To be fair, surging house prices have been a phenomenon all over the Western world in the past three decades. The UK, for example, has seen average house price growth of 400 per cent since 1995. But New Zealand leads the pack.

Was our new foreign-owned banking sector the primary cause of the long housing market boom? Well, nothing is that simple — but there is certainly a correlation between the sale of our banks and the dramatic acceleration of house prices. According to the Real Estate Institute of New Zealand, the median house price was about $120,000 in 1994. By the time the market peaked (post-Covid in late 2021), that median price was $925,000. In nominal terms that is huge. But what if we adjust for inflation? Well, it's still huge. Wages certainly haven't gone up 600 per cent since the mid-1990s. In inflation-adjusted terms — where we can imagine a 30-year-old from 1994 and a 30-year-old from 2023 with the same buying power at a supermarket — the price of a house now is still four times more than it was then.

I feel for young people because, frankly, the numbers involved just don't add up any more. According to work by Stats NZ (using the 2018 Census), home ownership in this country has reached a 70-year low.

HOME OWNERSHIP RATES

(Source: Stats NZ, https://www.stats.govt.nz/news/homeownership-rate-lowest-in-almost-70-years/)

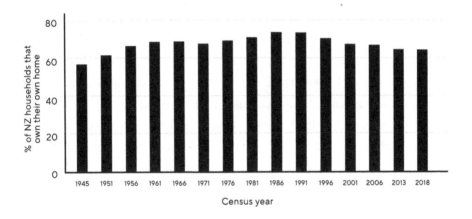

Avoiding the blame game

I was lucky to buy a house in the early 2000s (or lucky to have a wife who convinced me it was time we bought a house). Homes already seemed insanely expensive. My generation was priced out of the central Auckland suburbs we'd been used to renting in, and we headed west to wild new frontiers that, in hindsight, still seem central. But if I thought I'd missed the market boom, I was wrong. The really crazy leap in house prices happened through the 2010s. It changed the housing market in this country — possibly forever.

Although we've seen some rebalancing in the past couple of years, as prices have fallen and new multi-unit blocks have proliferated, we still can't begin to call housing affordable in anything like the way it was 30 or 40 years ago. Whether we ever get back to those kinds of levels might depend on whether we ever really want to.

Once you're on the housing ladder, rising prices create a sense of financial security and a wealth effect that New Zealand now relies on to boost economic confidence and keep things buoyant. Governments and the Reserve Bank know this and lean into it when it is required or, sometimes, when it is politically expedient. It is hard to win elections in this country when property prices are falling.

So, the big question is: how much financial security and paper wealth are those of us who own houses prepared to sacrifice for the next generation? Based on the evidence to date: not much.

I don't want to berate anyone in this chapter or generalise in a way that pitches one generation against another. It's not a simple issue, and it's important to acknowledge that property remains the most logical and accessible way for many Kiwis to make themselves financially secure. As I mentioned earlier, our property culture was born across generations when property was stable and secure. Kiwis didn't necessarily change or get greedier, but we were given access to capital, and we got better at buying and selling. We created conditions that made property investment even more lucrative.

We shouldn't demonise people for being landlords or buying a bach, or even just for obsessing about the value of their family home. Being able to buy and sell property is a basic principle of capitalism. Unless we go further to the left than most New Zealanders have ever wanted to, then we need to accept it is a normal part of life. But the idea that young people have to waste their twenties (and thirties, and sometimes their forties) living like monks to get on the property ladder is horrible to me.

I think we should be able to stand back and look at it all from a distance — to look at the economics. We can debate how we regulate and tax property, and we can encourage people to take a critical look at how the market works. And we should accept that attitudes to things will shift over time as new generations bring their lived experiences with them.

Nation of debt

One of the easiest ways to see the macro-economic problem that housing inflicts on our economy is to add up all our mortgages and just look at the eye-watering number. Then remember that we've borrowed almost all of that money from Australian banks. We send billions of dollars of interest payments across the Tasman every year.

That really doesn't help our current account, which is the difference between what the nation earns each year and what we spend. Countries that spend more than they earn have to cover the difference by borrowing even more, and it can be a dangerous spiral.

CURRENT ACCOUNT: WHAT GOES IN, WHAT GOES OUT

The current account is a bit like the country's cheque account. It measures a nation's business dealings with the rest of the world's — including exports and imports of goods and services, and all our financial transactions.

Another way of looking at the current account is like a company's general ledger: how much did we sell and how much did we buy last month? Ideally, New Zealand will sell more than it buys. But, like a lot of countries, we often don't. When that happens, we are running a current account deficit. The current account includes profits flowing in and out of the country. So, for example, the fact that the banks in New Zealand are largely foreign-owned means their multi-billion-dollar profits represent a big drain on our current account.

Sometimes economists will talk about the balance of trade, which is a subset of the current account, just looking at exports and imports. The current account is itself a subset of a broader measure of a nation's financial position with the rest of the world. That's called the balance of payments. The balance of payments includes the current account and the capital account. The capital account reflects the net change in a country's foreign assets and liabilities (or debt). If we run a current account deficit, we have to offset that shortfall by borrowing, which is added to the capital account.

Generally speaking, surpluses are good, and deficits are bad. If our current account deficit gets too big (usually measured as a percentage of GDP), then international creditors and ratings agencies start to look at us funny. They worry about our debt levels and ability to repay them. It's a bit like the way a bank might let you run a big overdraft if it can see you've got plenty of equity in your house. New Zealand gets cut plenty of slack by international creditors. We have a good track record of paying our debts. We have relatively stable export earnings because we produce food, and foreigners like to come here and look at our mountains.

Other wealthy nations like the US and UK also generally run current account deficits.

But we're a small country and our current account can swing quite wildly. Sometimes even one big purchase — like the navy buying a new frigate, or Air New Zealand buying a new plane — can blow out our monthly current account deficit. If we have a bumper dairy season and export prices are good, we sometimes run a current account surplus. But thanks to the foreign ownership of most of our major corporates — draining billions in profits out of the country every year — we are in deficit more often than not.

Can we keep running deficits forever? Well, as long as we keep borrowing to make up the deficit and keep paying the interest on our debt, then maybe, in theory. But once we fall too far behind, the costs of the debt start to rise and we'll start slowly slipping further into the red. If ratings agencies grow concerned, they'll downgrade our status, and that pushes up the interest rates that other countries will be prepared to offer us. Things can spiral out of control quickly as they did for Greece in 2010. As a strategy for long-term wealth creation, living in perpetual deficit leaves a lot to be desired.

If you add up all New Zealand's private debt — including housing, business, agricultural and consumer debt — it totals $562 billion at the time of writing. That's more than half a trillion dollars! And most of that — $352 billion as of September 2023 — is mortgage debt.

As a per capita ratio, our debt relative to our GDP is very high by global standards. As interest rates started to rise in early 2023, international economic research group Fitch Solutions put it this way: 'The impact of rising interest rates is significant for New Zealand given that household debt stood at 95.1 per cent of GDP, higher than the average of 72.9 per cent for advanced economies.'

That half-trillion is a number that worries Reserve Bank governors and finance ministers and overseas ratings agencies when they look at this country's financial stability risks. It should worry all of us. It's the reason our government can't afford to borrow enough to fund all the big new infrastructure projects we might like it to. Why we can't have a four-lane highway from one end of the country to the other, or an extensive high-speed rail network or another Auckland harbour crossing with walking and cycle lanes. And why we can't invest more in social programmes or even cut taxes (for those with other political preferences).

After all, our government debt — even after the Covid-era blow-out — is considered moderate by global standards at around 30 per cent of GDP. The US has a government debt-to-GDP ratio of about 150 per cent, the UK has 85 per cent and in Japan it runs at a whopping 260 per cent. But Japan can get away with it because its people are much better at saving, and they invest in their own government bonds. Some 90 per cent of the money that Japan owes, it owes to itself, rather than to foreign financial institutions. On that basis, Japan's balance sheet with the rest of the world isn't so bad.

The financial markets and rating agencies that decide whether we are a good risk for investment — and what our currency and government bonds are worth — look at our national debt in aggregate. Even the US and UK can run much higher government debt levels because their citizens are not so heavily in the red as we Kiwis are with our world-beating house prices.

Despite what some of the hawkish right-wing economic commentators might say about government borrowing, it's not really the politicians letting the side down. It's us — aided and abetted by a banking sector that, arguably, no longer has anything other than a financial stake in our national interest. I could berate the banks for taking advantage of us; that's a popular pastime. I certainly get frustrated with the extent to which they extract profit. And, like anyone, sometimes I get annoyed with their record of service and conduct.

But generally, my experience over the years is that the banks are pretty good corporate citizens, as far as that goes. They certainly invest in making sure New Zealanders have warm associations with their brands. They employ a lot of us, they sponsor good things like sport and rescue helicopters, and they are run by smart and friendly staff. That doesn't mean that as institutions they can't be ruthless.

Complaining about banks making money is a bit like blaming a wolf for eating your sheep. Wolves do what they do. It's on the shepherd to protect the sheep. Are we the sheep in that analogy? Is the government the shepherd? Or does that role belong to the Reserve Bank, which regulates the sector?

TRENDS IN BANK PROFITS

(Source: Reserve Bank of New Zealand, https://www.rbnz.govt.nz/hub/publications/financial-stability-report/2023/may-2023/fsr-may-23-special-topic-3)

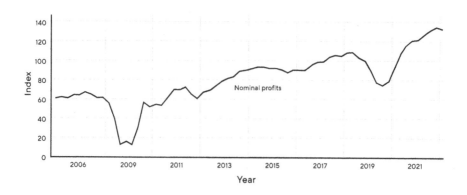

I think it's a bit easy to blame the policymakers. I think we've done this to ourselves. We sold the banks. We make the rules to regulate them, and we queue up to borrow from them. We took their money, and we used it to bid up the prices on our own houses. That has created plenty of paper wealth, but all the extra zeros on house prices just mean the next generation of Kiwis need to borrow more money . . . and around it goes.

In the past three decades, New Zealand's private debt levels have ballooned and Australian bank profits have soared.

Collectively are we any wealthier? I guess, if it all holds, then many of us are. Or at least we feel much more secure in the warm blanket of our housing equity. But the housing market is not a productive economic sector. It doesn't create new wealth by rearranging resources into better and more efficient systems, the way technology or manufacturing do.

The construction sector might argue there's an element of that to it. A building products company might manufacture a new cheaper, more weathertight type of wallboard. But simply selling the same houses over and over again, for ever larger sums, doesn't add real value to the country. It merely adds those zeros to our paper wealth — and our collective debt.

A house is just a home. If you own just the one, then its value is arbitrary because you always need to live somewhere. If the market goes well for you, it might give you options to trade down and buy somewhere smaller or cheaper, and bank some real returns.

Overall, though, it's a highly illiquid store of wealth: you can't access or redeploy it easily. You can't really use it for anything — except, perhaps, thanks to the banking system, borrowing more money to buy another house. Individually you do feel better off as your mortgage grows smaller and the value of your home grows larger. I won't deny this fills a very deep-seated human desire for security.

And if you are clever and motivated and can handle the paperwork and stress, you can buy a second property, and a third, and then you might start to create some real wealth for yourself. Assuming an ever-rising market, of course. That's been an assumption that took hold of New Zealand thinking on property through the 1990s and 2000s, although it probably has its roots much earlier. I once called it 'the great house price delusion'. We convinced ourselves that our housing market was a one-way bet. I don't think even the big post-Covid fall in prices and the arrival of higher interest rates has shifted that long-term cultural belief.

It is a market that will carry on for as long as New Zealand does. And I think the reality is that, no matter how much we wring our hands and worry about how our children and grandchildren will afford houses, this is how most Kiwis still like it.

Chapter 14

The only way is up: What really drives house prices?

Buy land, they're not making it anymore.
— Mark Twain

....

We spend a lot of time talking about how to make housing more affordable for future generations, but we always seem to get bogged down trying to identify the most important drivers of the housing market.

There are arguments about lack of supply: access to land, the costs of building, and planning red tape. There are arguments about things that drive excess demand, such as high immigration, low interest rates, and a loose tax regime that encourages speculative investment. For years, these arguments have created a policy gridlock. A cynic might think the entrenched positions have become an excuse, on both sides, for not properly fixing things.

Even when they are talking about making houses more affordable, politicians in both of New Zealand's major parties can never say out loud that they want the market to fall. It is considered political poison. Instead, there's a weird charade in which they talk about long periods of stability, even though the maths suggests it would require decades of stagnation for wages to catch up and bring our market back to the levels of affordability they have in Australia or the US.

There are people who'll try to tell you there's just one thing driving house prices. In my view those people are almost always pushing a political agenda. Society is more complex than that. There are always multiple factors to consider when we look at any market, not least because we have two sides of the market dynamic to consider: supply and demand.

We often see those who focus mostly on one side or the other divided along political lines. The left tend to favour regulation, seeing tax policy or more direct market restrictions as a way to influence demand. If you limit the profit people can make from property investment, then fewer will invest, and demand for houses will fall.

Those on the right see that kind of regulation as distorting the market and true value, which they believe creates instability. They're generally keener on supply-side solutions. They argue we should look at creating a thriving competitive market in which more houses are built more cheaply, until we reach a kind of socially acceptable equilibrium.

Supply-side factors tend to be those that affect the production and availability of housing. That might mean government policies and

NZ WAGES, RENT AND HOUSE PRICES 2001–2020
PERCENTAGE INCREASES IN AVERAGE WAGES, MEDIAN RENT AND MEDIAN HOUSE PRICES

(Source: *The Spinoff*, https://thespinoff.co.nz/money/26-01-2021/twenty-years-of-housing-costs-beating-wages-in-one-heinous-chart)

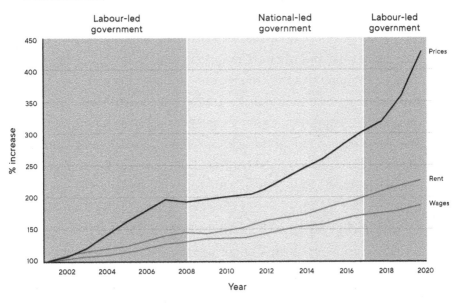

regulations that slow down the process of getting houses built — from applying for permission to getting building work signed off and sold. It's the stuff known by its detractors as 'red tape'. Demand-side factors are things like interest rates, population growth and immigration, all of which affect the number of buyers in a market. As should be clear by now, I'm a 'bit of both' kind of guy.

High on your own supply

Let's start by looking at the supply-side drivers. Are there enough houses? Is there enough land available to put them on? These are the fundamental questions.

In Europe or South East Asia, land might be scarce. But in most parts of the world, there's plenty of it. In New Zealand there is clearly no shortage of land. We have five and a bit million people living on a land mass with a footprint comparable to the UK, with its 67 million people, or Japan, with its 125 million. But we use a lot of it for farming and we're quite proud of having a fair bit of unspoiled natural beauty. That creates issues about where we are allowed to build houses.

Then there's the issue of the infrastructure that's required for people to live there, and importantly, who pays for that infrastructure. Given that the central or local government have to provide the roads and sewerage and power needed for households, they also maintain strict control over who can build what and where. They also have to factor in the views of the various communities they represent — not least because they'll be thrown out of power if their policies are too unpopular. After all, most people aren't too happy to see a skyscraper going up next door to them.

There's a balance to be struck between the value of retaining architectural character in a neighbourhood and ensuring the availability and affordability of homes. Even expensive and exclusive areas like central Auckland, Wellington and Queenstown need to accommodate people who work in important but often badly paid jobs.

If you put aside arguments of fairness, large areas where housing costs are prohibitive create problems because essential workers, like teachers and nurses, are effectively locked out. So, in the last few years pressure has been mounting to loosen regulations – to open up new land and to intensify housing on already developed land. Of all the issues that have contributed to New Zealand's long housing market boom, this is probably the one where we've made the most progress in the past few years. Thankfully, there has been some broad bipartisan support for urban intensification and less onerous zoning rules around the rural fringe of cities.

Unfortunately, land isn't the only supply-side issue. New Zealand hasn't done well at reining in construction costs, and our building products are expensive by international standards.

There are also some issues with geography and climate in this country. Our wet and windy weather means we need building products to be of a high standard. In the early 1990s a major regulatory failing, in the form of the Building Act 1991, ushered in a decade of poor-quality new builds – something now described as the leaky building crisis. According to a 2009 PwC report for the government, that debacle cost the country around $12 billion. It likely also significantly slowed the pipeline of new building as resources went to fixing up the leaky homes, something that may have contributed to the housing shortage through the next 10 years.

Worker shortages across the last few years of the pandemic and its aftermath haven't helped to keep down building labour costs, either. There have been efforts made to boost the number of locally trained builders and tradespeople needed to keep the sector thriving. Shortfalls have to be made up with immigrant labour, which becomes a catch-22 as new arrivals need somewhere to live, putting more pressure on demand.

Borrowing and boomers

Interest rates are such a hot topic that they have their own chapter coming up. However, the cost of borrowing also plays a specific role in determining the strength of the housing market, so we'll look at it here.

While interest rates are more directly linked to housing demand, they also play a part on the supply side. Property developers and construction companies need access to capital, so if the rates rise, we'll typically see the pace of new building and new property investment slow. When the cost of borrowing is low, conditions are generally good for a building boom, and that almost always goes hand in hand with good conditions for buyers. The difference is that the construction side often lags behind the buyer demand side; it takes longer to gear up and longer to slow down.

Some people argue that interest rates are the primary driver of demand in the housing market. Remember twentieth-century economist Milton Friedman's line: 'Inflation is always and everywhere a monetary phenomenon.' That can apply to house price inflation, too. We have had some periods of strong growth at times when rates have been relatively high – 2005 through 2008, for example. I guess monetarists like Friedman would argue that prices would have been even higher still without those rate rises.

I certainly don't doubt the power of money supply and interest rates to affect conditions for housing markets. But there is one even more basic demand-side driver: people. If you add more of them to an economy, they're going to want a place to live, and the demand will push prices up.

You can add more people via the birth rate. The postwar baby boomers have certainly driven demand at key moments in the history of New Zealand house prices. I suspect they played a part as first-home buyers in the strong market of the early and mid-1970s. They've showed up again as property investors since the mid-1990s. But since the turn of the millennium at least, the birth rate hasn't been a big driver of population growth, either in New Zealand or anywhere else in the wealthy end of the world.

The big driver of population growth has been immigration.

Welcome home

I like immigration, even though I don't especially like Dave Dobbyn songs about it. I like it for the diversity and culture (and great food) it brings to a nation. I like it because without it this country has a terrible shortage of workers in both skilled and unskilled jobs. I like it because the people who come are so full of passion and energy. It takes a huge effort and motivation to move across the world.

Often new immigrants will do jobs that more established citizens don't want, but (I'm generalising a bit now) they will put great effort into educating their children and encouraging them into more skilled professions. So, I'm in favour of quite a liberal approach to immigration.

But immigration is a sensitive topic because it risks inviting both unconscious and conscious xenophobia and racism. We need to be very careful not to target individuals and communities when we debate this issue.

New Zealand doesn't have a proud history in this regard. Take the example of Chinese immigration. In the 1890s (and the decades on either side), media and politicians whipped up public panic about the possibility of mass Chinese immigration, dubbed 'the yellow peril'. We passed very specific racist laws to make it extremely difficult for Chinese to get into New Zealand. It wasn't until the late 1980s that immigration laws based on country of origin were repealed in favour of a skills-based approach. That ushered in another wave of South East Asian arrivals in the 1990s and (surprise!) another era of racist panic about a supposed 'Asian invasion'.

The economic meltdown of the so-called Asian tiger economies in the late 1990s slowed that wave. But after signing a free trade agreement with China in 2008, we saw closer economic relations and another wave

NZ NET MIGRATION

(Source: Stats NZ, https://www.stats.govt.nz/news/net-migration-gain-driven-by-non-new-zealand-citizens/)

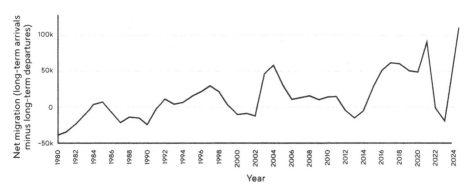

of immigration. When house prices soared dramatically in the mid-2010s, it generated additional public concern about Chinese people buying New Zealand houses. In opposition, the Labour Party released leaked real estate data in 2015 which showed a high proportion of houses were being sold to Chinese buyers, using their surnames as evidence.[14] The approach failed because the data they found had no way to distinguish the status of people with Chinese names: were they new migrants, residents, or descendants of the original wave of Chinese migration 100 years earlier?

I do know that, at that time, there was a lot of money from mainland China flowing into our housing market. Chinese contacts I had in Auckland would talk openly about the phenomenon, referring to 'uncles in Beijing' — effectively syndicates of older Chinese investors often buying through younger relatives in New Zealand on work visas. There were similar stories in Canada and Australia at the time. But there was never any hard data to suggest Chinese buyers were any more than a highly visible buyer group, influencing the market at the margins. The John Key years of 2008–16 also saw an influx of foreign buyers from the US, UK, Australia, Canada and India. We didn't seem to notice those buyers as much.

For all that, economics still requires that we look at things like the immigration rate dispassionately so we can measure it and its impact and put the right amount of resourcing and infrastructure in place. There's an argument that during the period between the GFC and the pandemic, we opened up our borders to more arrivals than we were able to plan and build for — and I think that has validity. But we can't blame the actual immigrants for the policy, or for our failure to invest in appropriate levels of infrastructure. And nobody seemed to mind the economic growth or 'rock star economy' status that accompanied the record immigration rates of 2016–17.

---

14   Claire Trevett, 'Little Backs Home-buyer Stats', *New Zealand Herald*, 13 July 2015, https://www. nzherald.co.nz/nz/little-backs-home-buyer-stats/ABK6QEA5IDXDEGL3HWKKNQPWVE/?c_ id=3&objectid=11479813.

In hindsight, the term 'Chinese buyer' was thrown around too loosely, with little regard to the fact that being Chinese is an ethnicity. It put the spotlight on people rather than economies. Highlighting the flow of capital from the People's Republic of China would have been more accurate and less encouraging of xenophobia.

Regardless, the Labour government — when it got into power in 2017 — moved to ban direct foreign investment in New Zealand residential property. By the time it passed legislation in 2018, the Chinese Communist Party in Beijing had also cracked down on the outflow of capital.

A new approach to immigration, developed by economists at the New Zealand Institute of Economic Research for the Productivity Commission, was picked up by the Labour government in 2018. It pushed back against high rates of immigration on the basis that cheap imported labour was allowing business to avoid investing in new technology and capital to improve productivity. The theory was that the wrong kind of immigration provides a tap of cheap, low-skilled workers for business and effectively keeps productivity and real wage growth low. Tougher immigration settings were brought into play. Perhaps the theory had merit, but the timing was terrible. The arrival of the pandemic shattered any sense of normality around borders and immigration.

With Covid-19 we saw a massive surge in Kiwis coming home, followed by a wave of departures as soon as borders reopened. New Zealand, like most of our advanced nation peers, ended up with labour shortages and falling house prices. Following that, through 2023, came another huge wave of immigrant arrivals. More recently, New Zealand's immigration records have tumbled again. Once we're through the effect of the pent-up demand created by the pandemic, a 'new normal' for immigration will likely be determined as much by economics around issues like labour shortages and house prices.

Ultimately, though — even through the immigration boom of 2015–18 — a big driver of the property-buying action remained Kiwi citizens investing in second and third homes. Ordinary New Zealanders made the obvious economic choice to leverage new-found equity in their family homes and become landlords. If anything, the power of New Zealand citizens and residents to drive a property boom was confirmed in the price surge that followed the arrival of Covid in 2020. We saw one of the biggest spikes in house prices during a period when there was no immigration at all.

With the profits on any capital gains being tax free, the question isn't why do it? The question is, why wouldn't you?

Taxing questions

In most countries we compare ourselves to, any profit made on selling property is taxed. Sometimes the family home is exempt, sometimes not. But if you buy an investment property and later sell it at a profit, you will have to pay a tax on that profit.

Professional property investors in this country are quick to point out they do pay tax on their capital gains. If being a property investor is primarily what you do for a living, you are expected to declare profits — just like any business. But for most 'mum and dad' investors who have a second or third property, capital gains are treated as incidental, as long as they're not a primary source of income and you don't buy and sell too frequently. There are 'bright line tests' which set limits on how long you have to own a property before you are exempt from paying tax on gains from selling it.

The bright line test was first introduced by National in 2015 at two years; it was extended to five years in 2018 by Labour and again to 10 years from 2021 (excluding new builds). For many Kiwis that's still no deterrent to acquiring property as a long-term investment — especially if it's aimed at funding a comfortable retirement or passing on wealth to children.

Our lack of a broad-based, comprehensive capital gains tax in the country has been very contentious. Many, particularly on the left, see it as a primary driver of New Zealand's property-obsessed investment culture. Most economists agree that tax settings do drive behaviour. Investment capital tends to follow the most lucrative, tax-efficient pathways.

DEATH[15] AND TAXES . . . AND *FERRIS BUELLER'S DAY OFF*

Those of us who grew up on 1980s teen movies have already had something called the Laffer curve explained to us by the long-suffering economics teacher in the movie *Ferris Bueller's Day Off.* It is an economic theory that changed the way we think about tax.

With its dazed and stupefied kids staring into space and drooling on their desks, the scene is meme-worthy to this day. But hardly anyone remembers the lecture the teacher was giving, which was a comparison between post-Depression Keynesian economic policy and the contemporary (in the mid-1980s) debate about neoliberal low tax policies.

Even at the time, when it dominated political thinking, the Laffer curve was controversial, underpinning what became known as 'trickle-down economics'. It's long been recognised that if you tax people too much, they become less productive; even in ancient times, kings noticed that starving workers weren't at their best. In the 1970s, an economist called Arthur Laffer quantified it all with a curve that plotted economic growth, with 100 per cent taxation at one end and zero taxation at the other. He argued you could actually boost economic growth by cutting taxes — that the optimum point for growth was at the low-tax end of the curve.

The theory is that governments can collect more tax by setting lower tax rates because the economy will be more efficient, and companies will make bigger profits — more than making up the difference. The idea was famously dismissed as 'voodoo economics' by George Bush Snr in 1980 when he was running against Ronald Reagan for the Republican presidential

---

15   Sorry, I didn't get to death.

nomination. He lost, and Reaganomics swept the world.

The idea remains hotly disputed in mainstream economics, and Laffer's low-tax arguments are broadly out of favour these days. After the GFC and the big public bailouts the financial sector needed, people became a little more sceptical. I don't think that, conceptually, the curve itself is wrong. Too much tax can be a disincentive to invest and create wealth, and low taxes can do the opposite — especially in a world where business is global and can go where the tax treatment is most generous.

Rather than disputing the Laffer curve per se, the left and right wing are really just arguing about where the optimal point on it is. You can find numerous studies debunking the extreme low-tax version of Laffer's theory. But it still forms the basis of policy in right-wing parties like the Republicans in the US and ACT in New Zealand.

In 2018, the Labour government commissioned former finance minister Sir Michael Cullen to lead a Tax Working Group to look at how a capital gains tax might work. The group came back with a comprehensive plan to overhaul New Zealand's tax system in a way that was ultimately neutral in terms of the government's revenue take. The family home would have been exempt, but profits on all other capital gains, including shares and other business investments, would have been taxable. The pay-off would have been sizeable income tax cuts for most people.

For a while, it looked like it might actually happen. But Labour's coalition partner, New Zealand First, was vehemently opposed to it. Ultimately, facing a strident backlash from business and property investment groups, as well as some trepidation from many ordinary Kiwis, Prime Minister Jacinda Ardern ruled it out. In fact, she ruled it out at any stage while she was prime minister, a move that underscored just how entrenched New Zealand's property investment mentality is politically. Perhaps we'll regret that move one day.

In the short term — as with immigration — the harsh economic reality of the pandemic put the capital gains tax debate quickly in the rear-view mirror. The housing market finally went into reverse from late 2021. It seems unlikely that we'll ever get a clean read on what really killed the beast.

With the exception of a capital gains tax, all the other drivers on the supply and demand side seemed to have finally lined up. Stimulus unleashed by the government and Reserve Bank fuelled a pandemic housing boom. Then, as inflation spiralled, the policy was thrown into reverse. Monetary policy settings tightened fast. Interest rates rose while the immigration rate remained low. Government regulations designed to slow housing investment — like the removal of tax deductions and the extension of bright line limits — made investing less lucrative.

Meanwhile, the construction boom kept rolling, fed by increased land supply and looser zoning rules.

Throughout 2023, interest rates kept rising as the Reserve Bank looked to reduce demand in the economy and get inflation back down to its target of below three per cent. The number of consents for new homes declined from record highs, and from a pandemic stimulus peak at $1.06 million by January 2022, the average New Zealand house price dropped about 16 per cent — to around $888,000 in May 2023.[16] Since then, there have been signs of progress on housing affordability. By September 2023 there was a record proportion (26.4 per cent) of first-home buyers in the total market, according to property analysts CoreLogic.

But we also saw immigration bounce back dramatically after the reopening of borders. A record net gain of 118,000 new migrants was added to the population in the 12 months prior to September 2023. That helped put a floor under the decline in the housing market. From the middle of the year, prices plateaued.

At the time of writing, a new, supposedly property-friendly, National-led government was expected to relax investor rules, and interest rates

---

16   https://www.qv.co.nz/price-index/

were expected to track back down. This led many pundits to predict we'll see another cycle of house price growth coming in the next year or so.

With neither major political party prepared to consider significant changes to the taxation of capital gains on property, and New Zealand once again relying on high levels of migration to ease skill shortages and prop up economic growth, it looks very much like the historic patterns of the past 30 or 40 years will repeat for the next generation at least.

What that means for young Kiwis isn't clear. But it doesn't appear that getting on the property ladder is about to get any easier.

Hopefully it is clear by this point that I won't be offering a guide to buying and selling property. I simply don't have any experience in it. But after years spent studying markets, I can advise with some certainty that it's good to buy things for less than you can sell them for, or sell things for more than you bought them for. Either way, you won't go too far wrong. Just don't get caught with too much debt at the wrong time. The market only has to go backwards for a while and interest rates only need to spike briefly to blow things up if your timing is all wrong.

Let's take a deeper look now at interest rates and what drives them.

Chapter 15

Debt dilemmas: Fixing, floating and the price of borrowing

May you live in interesting times.
— Ancient Chinese proverb

....

What's going to happen to interest rates? That's the big one when it comes to BBQ questions. It seems a simple enough thing to ask. It's almost always because people have a fixed-term mortgage that's about to roll over and they have to choose a new term. But actually, it's a question that takes us deep into the cold heart of the financial system. It's a leap into a world of investment that we seem to find far more comfortable than that of shares and bonds and other financial products.

I guess we feel that houses are solid and tangible; we can kick the walls and inspect the guttering. It feels like a market that might also be a bit more stable and grounded, sheltered from the arcane vagaries of global finance. I suspect we're kidding ourselves.

Anyway, let's take a more in-depth look at the costs of borrowing.

How long should I fix?

It's a weird quirk of New Zealand life that homeowners — and that's a lot of us — like to take a punt on short-term interest rates, effectively betting on the markets as if we were hedge funds. In fact, Reserve Bank data shows that more than 85 per cent of Kiwis choose to fix their mortgage rates for a set period at a set price, rather than just float along with the market rate.

Around the world, habits vary. In the US, people mostly fix their mortgages for a much longer period (30-year terms are quite normal) and then they forget about it. In Australia, only 20–30 per cent of people fix at all; they mostly go with the ups and downs of the market. So, the typical Aussie BBQ question might be: should I fix or float? This side of the Tasman it's almost always: how long should I fix for?

In New Zealand, most of us take new short or long positions every year. Or every two years, or six months, or five years, depending on how we think the market might go. We seem to spend a lot of time worrying about it. But we also seem to love it, because we keep doing it – even though, as a financial strategy, it doesn't really work. Just take a look at the profits the Australian banks (that lend us the money) are making. In 2022 they made about $7 billion in New Zealand, according to KPMG.[17]

So, who's really winning?

Like gamblers, we convince ourselves that we can beat the bank and somehow get a bargain on our interest rate if we can just make a clever enough decision, and if the market moves in the direction we hope it does. Let me just throw it out there now: this is complete nonsense. Nothing I can tell you at a BBQ is going to help you beat the banks. Perhaps, if you do it professionally and train yourself by placing bets all day/every day, you might get good enough to win more than you lose. But the odds are you're a regular homeowner like me and three million or so other Kiwis, and you're just rolling the dice once a year or so.

I know I sound cynical. I'm certainly not opposed to making an informed choice about what to expect when it comes to borrowing costs. I hope you'll read the business pages of the *Herald* and the blogs and websites and use them as a guide. But I'm highly sceptical of the notion – often sold to us by the personal finance industry – that there's some magic formula which can help you crack the system and pay lower rates than everybody else. There really isn't.

Over the years, I've had the privilege of many long conversations with central bankers who are about as knowledgeable as it gets, and the first

17   John Kensington, 'FIPS Banks: Review of 2022', KPMG, https://kpmg.com/nz/en/home/insights/2023/03/fips-banks-review-of-2022.html.

thing they'll tell you is that they can't predict the future. Central bankers have to make very big judgement calls about where to set rates to make sure the economy is stable. If we extend the gambling analogy, they are like the high rollers, the elite who are really good at what they do. And even they can't always get it right.

The problem is that they have to deal with the financial markets like everyone else. And the market is always right — even if it shouldn't be. The markets that central banks have to bet against are global debt markets. These are usually called bond markets.

BONDS: MORE FIREPOWER THAN 007

There's a case to be made that bond markets are the most powerful political force in the world. Obviously military might trumps most things, but even an army needs cash.

Bond markets control the world's debt — in fact, they are sometimes described as debt markets, because they represent the bulk of traded debt. And the world runs on debt. Bonds are issued by governments to raise national debt. They're also issued by large companies. The idea is that governments and corporates are stable entities we can trust to repay the debt at a set interest rate and a set time.

With a value of more than US$130 trillion, bond markets represent more money than actually exists in the world. They're roughly twice as big as global share markets, depending on how you do the counting. And because these markets control the price of borrowing for nations, they can effectively sink an economy if the world's traders turn against it.

James Carville, political strategist for Bill Clinton, made the point with a famous line back in 1993: 'I used to think that if there was reincarnation, I wanted to come back as the President or the Pope or as a .400 baseball hitter. But now I would want to come back as the bond market. You can intimidate everybody.'

Carville — who also coined Clinton's successful campaign slogan in 1992 ('It's the economy, stupid') — was making the point that bond markets rule the world. They are so important that their pricing is considered one of the best indicators of which way the economy is going to go. In other words, people think they can predict recessions. So it's good to understand how they work even if you don't trade in them.

Unfortunately, understanding them is perpetually difficult because they have an extra mental step in their pricing. After a bond is issued it can be traded on a secondary market. This reprices them based on how much interest they have left to pay and how that interest rate compares with new rates on offer. It also prices them for risk, as a company or country's fortunes may rise and fall across the duration of the bond's term. That means that there's a counterintuitive aspect to the way that bond markets trade. There's an inverse relationship between the price and the yield (or interest) offered on a bond. It's a bit like backing a trailer (something I've never really mastered).

Put simply, when the general cost of borrowing in the economy goes down, and interest rates fall, the price of a bond goes up. That's because bonds usually offer a fixed rate of return for a set period of time. If interest rates rise, then that pre-fixed rate won't look so attractive compared with other new bond issues. The bond price will fall. If interest rates fall, then the fixed rate on that bond will start to look very good and the price of the bond will rise.

There are other factors in the price equation — such as how long the bond has left until it matures. In fact, there's a complicated mathematical formula to work it all out. I won't try to explain it here.

If you like a challenge, this is what it looks like:

Price of bond = (C / (1 + r)^1) + (C / (1 + r)^2) + ... + (C + FV / (1 + r)^n)

I'm not even going to attempt to decode that!

Big investors understand it, though, and most of them — including KiwiSaver funds — like bonds because of their stability compared with that of shares. They can be used to offset riskier investments.

Bonds offer lower risk and lower returns. Except sometimes. Generally, interest rates are pretty stable because they are well-signalled by the central banks that set wholesale rates. But if they rise quicker than expected — like they did when inflation hit the post-pandemic world in 2022 — then bond investors can take big losses.

Sometimes bond markets get weird and start doing the opposite of what they should. When they do, financial commentators like me freak out and start talking about inverted yield curves and recessions.

An inverted yield curve is considered one of the best predictors of recession. An example might be if the yield (or interest) on the five-year US Treasury Bond fell below the yield on the three-year bond. That means bond investors are getting paid more to hold shorter-term US government debt than they get for holding it for a longer term. (That's not the way it's supposed to work. It's supposed to be riskier — with a better return — to hold debt for longer, which is why banks offer better interest on longer term deposits.) An inversion tells us the long-term outlook isn't great, and that markets think things are going to get worse, not better.

So, going back to James Carville's point, politicians can make promises and plans for their economy, but they don't mean a thing if the bond markets decide to tell a different story.

Countries like the US and China are especially powerful, and so if you are the US Federal Reserve or Bank of China, you carry some serious weight on the world stage. New Zealand? Not so much. So, if central bankers are the high rollers in this scenario, think of the markets as the casino, the 'house'. Feel free to think about them as sharply dressed players, like Robert De Niro in Martin Scorsese's *Casino*, or as the decrepit mafia bosses sitting in some squalid basement in Kansas City. We all have different thoughts on how ruthless and organised these market bosses really are. But they don't care. They set the price of things, and they do it in a way that almost nobody can control. Even though they are playing the game with a large chunk of our collective retirement savings.

The central banks have influence. They get to set the starting price for borrowing in their home market, but markets can move against them. If a country gets into trouble by defaulting on debt or straying wildly from orthodox economic policies, then central banks lose control. You can push your official state interest to zero (or lower), but if the world decides you're a risk, your cost of borrowing will rise.

Plenty of countries have had their economies tanked by international debt markets at various times. They include Argentina, Greece and Venezuela, as well as 1920s Germany and even the US when the GFC hit in 2008. Mostly, though, in compliant and careful little countries like New Zealand, they don't move against us. We try to stay within boundaries that don't cause any major ructions on markets.

Why rates move

It's worth pausing here to consider again why rates move around and how central banks control them. It all comes back (again) to monetary policy, which, as you will recall, we use to control the amount of money circulating in the economy. Too much money in the economy creates extra demand and pumps up prices. If prices rise too fast and incomes don't, then we all get poorer.

Thanks to the after-effects of the pandemic stimulus, we no longer have to head for the history books or stretch our minds back to the

1980s for examples of this. Excess money supply through 2022 saw inflation rise, hitting Kiwis hard in the back pocket. Consumer price inflation peaked at 7.3 per cent in the June 2022 quarter.

It's hard to do business, or even run a household, if you can't be sure what a dollar will buy next month. As already mentioned, in extreme cases — like the hyperinflation that hit Germany in the 1920s — things spiral out of control and the public loses confidence in the value of money.

Central banks have the government licence to print money and it's their job to make sure there's the right amount in circulation to ensure the economy is stable. In New Zealand, the most powerful tool the Reserve Bank has is its ability to set the Official Cash Rate (see page 121). It's the baseline for interest rates, the starting point for the banks before they add their margins.

If the OCR drops, mortgage rates usually follow. That's good news for homeowners, as it effectively puts cash back in their pockets. If it rises, then retail rates will follow, and it will take cash out of mortgage-holders' pockets. It's not all about mortgage-holders, even though that's the group we tend to obsess over. Higher rates encourage saving, which further restricts the money supply.

The cost of borrowing is also used as an incentive or disincentive for business to expand. So, if the money supply is plentiful and interest rates are low, businesses will be encouraged to invest in growth and hire more staff. That's why central banks used low rates, and even printed extra money, to keep economies from crashing after the GFC and again through the Covid-19 pandemic.

But it's the cost of debt for homeowners that media tends to focus on. That's where the bulk of the interest (so to speak) lies.

Placing a bet . . . or forging a strategy

Anyway, let's now come back to you: making your mortgage rate call, throwing your handful of chips on the table for an annual or biennial spin of the roulette wheel.

As you ponder whether to fix for one year or two, think about the advice I could give you around the BBQ. Compare it to all the data that is being pored over every day by teams of economists for the major banks. Then think about how all the economic analysis being produced by bank economists is being processed and actioned by steel-hearted traders. These are people who have no fears about moving hundreds of millions of dollars around in seconds, based on a combination of knowledge and old-fashioned intuition.

Good luck.

Just as it should be at a casino, it's obvious that, on aggregate, we're not beating the retail banks or the money markets. That doesn't mean you can't get lucky. But most of us only really nail it with spot-on fixed rate picks a few times across the length of a mortgage. There'll be a few times where we get it wrong and kick ourselves and call it a learning experience, and then there'll be plenty more where it's kind of hard to say how we did. On the plus side, if you have savings and investments, even a KiwiSaver retirement fund, then you'll be collecting some of those winnings by way of interest or dividends.

Economic knowledge might not help you beat the market, but it will help you contextualise your decision-making. You could pick a sensible position that reflects a broad view about the direction the economy is going. Or you could also choose a higher-risk position — with more potential upside. We'll look at risk and investing in the next chapter.

When people ask me what's going to happen with interest rates, what I really want to say is that they will go up and down and banks will keep making money. That's the real answer to the most popular question in New Zealand economics. It's a bit of a cop-out, though, and it's too negative. And I want to get invited back to more BBQs. So, let's run through it again in a less cynical way and ponder the best interest rate strategy for you.

Obviously, what you don't want to do when you set your mortgage rate is exactly the wrong thing. That could cost you a lot of money. At best, you'd feel bad about yourself. At worst, you'd find yourself struggling to make mortgage payments. Actually, if we're talking the worst-worst, the bank might force you to sell your home. (For a more positive take, this seems like a pretty grim start.) Unless something really weird happens, like a war or a pandemic (imagine that!), economists have a general idea about the direction the world is travelling and the parameters for interest rates in the near future. So, some knowledge about what's going on in the economy can help you avoid bad choices.

As I mentioned earlier, we Kiwis have a cultural pride thing about trying to pick our own rate — like mowing our own lawns or building our own deck. It's considered normal. And another thing you really don't want to be is a weirdo, right? Because the market is so geared towards people choosing short- and medium-term fixed rates, that's where the best deals tend to end up in this country. It's the biggest part of the market, so it's where the most competition between banks happens, which means it's where there is the most price pressure. And yeah, trying to pick the interest rate market might be masochistic and delusional, but it can also be kind of fun.

If you are spending a lot of time in your head worrying about whether to fix for 18 months or two years, at least you aren't worrying about your health, or your kids, or your marriage . . . or death . . . or whatever. So, you're going to get in there and play the game. Even though you can't beat them, you're going to join them. That's fine. So, what do you need to know?

First, let's nail the real purpose of fixing a price. What we're trying to do with fixing and then refixing at regular intervals is balance security with flexibility. Rather than look at fixing a mortgage rate as a way to save money, think of it as a way to avoid stress and potential financial ruin. Think of it as a kind of insurance. That's why big companies fix their borrowing costs or energy prices and even their international currency needs. Companies want predictable prices so they can keep expenditure stable and focus on growing and earning more revenue and reinvesting in the business, and so on.

In theory, we should expect to pay for the privilege of financial security, as we would for any other service. Someone else is taking the risk and we are locking in certainty. But when we stare at the myriad mortgage rates offered by retail banks, we still face a difficult and personal economic choice. We have to make a decision about where we want to set the balance between flexibility and security — because it's a trade-off, like so much in economics.

Naturally, it's important to put your personal circumstances front and centre of any choices you make about locking in your mortgage rate. And to give you useful financial advice, I'd need to know more about you so I could factor in things that are important to your lifestyle — such as your age, for starters. How much security do you have around your cashflow? What's your income and is it secure? Are you in a small business where work and income can fluctuate wildly from one year to the next? Or are you in a corporate job where the salary is good, but you could be erased in a brutal HR cull in the next business downturn? Perhaps you're a teacher or a nurse where the salary isn't so huge, but your employment prospects are steady and secure for life. All these things should affect the way you set your mortgage to some extent.

That's why professional financial advice is a serious business done face to face by people with certificates on the wall.

What do I do?

If you publish anything that answers questions about your personal approach to finance, you have to include a disclaimer warning people not to construe what you're saying as financial advice. It all seems a bit artificial, sometimes, like the obligatory encores at rock concerts. But for this next bit, I really mean it. This isn't meant to be a formula to follow; think of it more as a case study from which you could create your own formula.

Anyway, for the record, this is what makes me feel most comfortable. When my mortgage term is up and I have to refix, I take the best available rate at the more short-term end of the market. That's what most of us do when we buy anything else in our lives: we take the best price on offer. And that's usually a shorter fixed term — which, as I mentioned, is where the best deals tend to land in New Zealand, based on the weight of numbers. There have been times when floating rates were lower, but not many since the 1990s.

RETAIL MORTGAGE RATES – 1998 TO 2024

(Source: Reserve Bank of New Zealand, https://www.rbnz.govt.nz/statistics/key-statistics/housing)

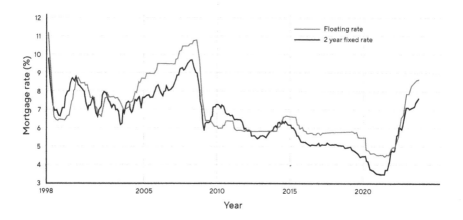

By staying on six-month or one-year terms, I still ride the ups and downs of the interest rate market. It also provides a bit of stability. I do think about things like the market consensus on where rates are headed, but only as far out as six months or a year. After that, neither the economists nor the markets have a good track record of picking what will happen. Events are too unpredictable. By all means go for terms of two, three or five years if what you want is certainty. But I reckon by the time you get to the preferred Kiwi fixed rate of two years, you're into territory where the forecasts are becoming a roll of the dice.

Oh, and to hedge my bets further I have split my mortgage in two so I can have one part longer term and one shorter and keep them rolling off at different times. Over the past few years, I've become even more basic and shifted to having both parts staggered on 12-month terms – so one mortgage is rolling over every six months.

We should acknowledge we all have a personal bias forged in the economic events we've lived through. For me, it was getting burned a couple of times (between the GFC and the pandemic) fixing for longer terms at higher rates than I needed to, because everybody in the market said rates were about to rise. Through the decade after the GFC, we had several false starts with expectations of interest rate rises. People assumed we'd see a more rapid return to more 'normal' elevated rates after the emergency lows of the GFC.

One of the other mistakes people make is thinking there *is* some kind of normal for interest rates. They really are just what they are and reflect the kind of history we are living through. If rates are high, then it is bad news for us as borrowers. But higher rates also likely mean higher inflation, which means the price of everything is rising fast — hopefully including your wages. If rates and inflation are high, the real value of your debt should be shrinking — which is good news for you and bad news for the bank.

There are swings and roundabouts, and across the lifetime of a mortgage it balances out more than you think. Which is probably why Americans and Brits don't bother with all the palaver. What's crucial is to keep making your mortgage payments. You need to be sure, if you fix a short-term or floating rate, that you won't be caught out if it rises fast. Fixing longer might cost more, but it means you have less to worry about.

In the end, what you really have to decide is this: how much risk are you prepared to take? What is your capacity to deal with uncertainty, and how much will you worry?

Chapter 16

How worried do you want to be?

Take calculated risks.
That is quite different from being rash.
— General George Patton

....

How worried should I be about . . .?

That's the starting premise for a lot of the questions I get about the economy. How worried should we be about the global banking crisis? Or about the housing market, or the recession, or the national debt? As I mentioned in the introduction, economics offers up plenty of things to worry about and plenty of reasons to worry about them. But there is something much deeper to understanding how much you want to worry about money. In many ways it goes to the heart of our relationship with it.

If you care enough about money (whether through need or desire) to endure worrying about it, then you're likely to have a higher appetite for risk in the financial decisions you make. The financial sector puts a lot of effort into assessing and understanding and managing risk these days. But risk appetite is an individual thing. (It really puts the personal in personal finance.) Some of us are more comfortable with risk-taking than others. Are you a keen skydiver or high-stakes gambler? Are you an active share trader, or are you content with a conservative KiwiSaver fund?

Whatever your threshold for danger, it's probably different to mine. It's probably unique to you. It may even be genetic. A study published in 2019 found 124 genetic variants associated with risky behaviour.[18] The researchers were keen to emphasise that no single variant was meaningful on its own, which hints at just how complex an area of human behaviour this is. And when you overlay all our cultural and learned behaviour on so many genetic factors, you can see why — despite all the research — investors, businesses, markets and whole economies keep getting underdone by poor risk management.

'Being willing to take risks is essential to success in the modern world,' said study co-author Abraham Palmer, PhD, professor of psychiatry and vice chair for basic research at UC San Diego School of Medicine. 'But we also know that taking too many risks, or not giving enough weight to the consequences of risky decisions, confers vulnerability to smoking, alcoholism and other forms of drug addiction.'

In other words, when it comes to worrying, there is a Goldilocks zone: we need to worry just the right amount. But finding that zone isn't easy, so one of the keys to a good relationship with money is understanding your own risk appetite. Part of doing that is being self-aware and recognising any biases you have.

You're probably not as good at risk assessment as you think. But if you are any good, you should already understand how bad you are. Recognising our inadequacies at assessing risk is the key theme of *Risk Intelligence* by Dylan Evans, which was a revelation to me when I read it back in 2011. It's really a book on behavioural psychology and as such is blissfully free of business jargon. It didn't prompt me to change my behaviour and begin winning on the stock markets, but as a primer into the academic field of risk management it is fascinating.

Risk assessment is at the heart of all good decision-making, and that includes investment choices. It is a fundamental skill for business success. Evans defines risk intelligence as 'the ability to estimate

18   Heather Buschman, 'Large Study Identifies Genetic Variants Linked to Risk Tolerance and Risky Behaviors', press release, UC San Diego Health, https://health.ucsd.edu/news/press-releases/2019-01-14-large-study-identifies-genetic-variants-linked-to-risk-tolerance-risky-behaviors/.

probabilities accurately'. He argues that it is a distinct intellectual ability — like emotional intelligence or memory. Some people seem to be born with it. Certainly, the very wealthy often have that skill at the core of their success. You've got to 'know when to hold 'em and know when to fold 'em', as Kenny Rogers would say.

It's all about achieving the right balance. Overconfidence is a trap that sinks many people in business and investing. But not acting is no good, either. You won't get rich unless you take risks. If you just want slow, steady returns, that's what savings accounts are for.

Hart of the matter

I once asked Graeme Hart, New Zealand's richest individual, about the risky nature of his highly leveraged business strategies. He told me he had a serious aversion to risk. That's why he invests in low-risk businesses, such as packaging and staple foods, which are some of the least volatile industry sectors. 'I'm pretty confident that you're going to eat your toast in the morning regardless,' he said. 'And you're going to put butter on it and you're going to have a glass of milk.'

To be fair, Hart was probably underplaying some of the risk he takes, and I'll come back to that. But what he does have is a very good understanding of how much risk he is taking at any given time. He invests big, but he doesn't speculate.

Back in 2003, at the age of 47, Hart was making headlines as New Zealand's first billionaire. He is now estimated to be worth around US$9 billion, although it's hard to say for sure because he and his business interests have long since departed from the stock exchange. The business empire, held together by private equity firm Rank Group, is owned outright by Hart, along with a small group of his family and closest colleagues. I guess he figures it's all less risky that way.

Hart absolutely did take risks early on when he made the leap from running businesses on a relatively small local scale in New Zealand, to Australia, then on to Europe and the US. As business columnist Brian Gaynor wrote in the *Herald* in 2003, Hart had 'a little luck but most of his high-risk acquisitions have been carefully thought out and, most importantly, he has been able to correct his mistakes without incurring major long-term damage to himself'.

Hart's back story is compelling. He left school at 16 and worked as a panel-beater and tow-truck driver. Later, he started his own printing business, built it up, sold out and bought into a catering and equipment hire business, amalgamating several companies along the way. Even though Hart started on the streets, he was smart enough to go back to school in the mid-1980s when he saw the financial stuff was getting complex, doing a Master of Business Administration degree at Otago University. He listed Rank Group in 1987, narrowly avoiding the boom and bust of the big share market crash.

Hart got his big step-up from the once-in-a-lifetime opportunity of the fire sale of New Zealand government state assets through the 1980s and early 1990s. In 1989, aged 34, he successfully bid for the Government Printing Office (GPO). He paid $23 million — more than $20 million below its book value. So, Hart had some luck, although, Gaynor also notes, he demonstrated 'remarkable skills' in turning Rank from a small company that raised just $2.75 million from the public into a $300 million Australasian retail and printing group.

In 1991, Hart bought bookseller and stationer Whitcoulls for $71 million (with $53 million of that debt-funded). After a series of further acquisitions, he privatised the group, selling it to Blue Star stationery in 1997. Then in June that year, Hart made a big change in direction and purchased a 20 per cent shareholding in Australian food group Burns Philp. He paid just A$2.50 a share — a total of A$260 million — and his timing was terrible. Or at least, it looked that way at the time; Hart might disagree now.

Burns Philp's share price tanked. It was full of overvalued assets; its costs were too high, and it wasn't making enough money. Within months, Hart's shares were almost worthless, and the company was in the hands of bankers. But against the odds he traded his way out.

Hart methodically turned the company around and followed it up by purchasing NZ Dairy Foods, the country's second-biggest consumer dairy company. Then he launched an even more audacious $2.2 billion bid for Australasian food giant Goodman Fielder in 2003. (That was about when I started reporting on Hart's business interests, and he gave me three lengthy interviews.) He restructured Goodman Fielder before relaunching it on the stock market in a move that pushed his net wealth well past the billion-dollar mark.

From there, Hart shifted to the next most predictable thing he could find: food packaging. He repeated his formula of borrowing big – taking on debt that would terrify mere mortals – to buy on low-risk assets, and backing himself to make them more profitable.

He's clearly very good at picking his people and managing relationships. 'I'm no walk-on-water guy,' he told me in 2005. 'People see my face and they tote up the money, and they think lucky, fabulous, all that. But the fact is, without my team I'd be wheel-spinning and I wouldn't get any traction.' And he added, 'There is a huge family value. We work and we play with our family and there's nothing much in between. We don't play a lot of golf.'

Of course, he must also be smart and lucky and have an obsession for detail. But it's rare that an entrepreneur like Hart suffers from a nervous disposition. The fact that he is so relaxed about having such enormous debts hanging over his head has to go with a certain kind of character. For some reason, the richest people often seem to share an attitude to risk that might also be found in mountain climbers or racing car drivers.

If Hart has some genius that other smart, hard-working charismatic businesspeople don't, it seems to be tied up with his innate ability to assess and manage risk.

SURVIVORSHIP BIAS

Are billionaires really superhuman geniuses? Or have they cracked a secret code of success that we could emulate if we just followed their advice? It's probably a bit of both. But two things are certain. One is that even if *anyone* can do it, *everyone* can't. The other is that if anyone can do it, someone inevitably will.

There's an evolutionary aspect to entrepreneurial success that people don't like to acknowledge. It's a logical fallacy called survivorship bias. According to financial website Investopedia.com, it occurs 'when only the winners are considered while the losers that have disappeared are not considered'.

In a world based on the survival of the fittest, we only get to observe the fittest. We see the examples that thrive, and not the ones that don't. This can apply to stocks when we assess the performance of successful viable firms and ignore those that failed and disappeared.

Another real-world example is in the wartime work done by Hungarian statistician Abraham Wald, who was asked to analyse damage to returning Allied bombers to work out how they could be better protected. The military's original plan was to add extra armour to the areas of returning planes that showed the most damage. Accounting for survivorship bias, Wald deduced that it was the areas on returning planes which had sustained *no* damage that required more protection. That's because the planes that took hits in those areas had not returned.

Survivorship bias can equally apply to business success for individuals. The difference between a billionaire and a bankrupt might hang on one key piece of luck or timing. If a self-made billionaire dropped out of college (like Mark Zuckerberg) or made their first million in highly leveraged business takeovers (like Hart), that isn't really evidence for anything. I don't think that means we should ignore the advice of successful people — in fact, I'll share advice from Warren Buffett later — but we live in a world that celebrates success, and that makes us all vulnerable to survivorship bias.

Risky business

There are different kinds of risk. It's not just about the specifics of an activity and judging the likelihood of success or failure. It also involves assessing the stakes and the consequences of success and failure.

As Graeme Hart was building his empire through the 1980s–2000s, he was looking at risk differently to many of his peers who got caught up in speculative investments, often involving property deals. Hart traded through business cycles as whole industries collapsed around him. He created a world in which he had control over the variables, where there were fundamentally fewer things that could go wrong – even though the stakes were high if they did.

At the time I was covering Hart's business most actively, I used to ride a motorcycle to the office. So, back then, the best analogy to risk that I could find was in my decision-making around the safest route to work. Riding a motorcycle on Auckland's busy streets is probably statistically more dangerous than skydiving into the office. But I had a choice: I could take the motorway or use the ordinary streets. After some hair-raising experiences, I worked out the motorway was far safer, as the traffic all moved in one direction and there was no one coming out from side streets or pulling mad U-turns. But, of course, if I did crash at high speed I was far more likely to die. The stakes were too high on the motorway, so despite my bias – an aversion to crashing at all – I went back to braving the side streets.

(In the end, a couple of minor crashes on the side streets convinced me to ditch motorbike riding altogether. I'm yet to take up skydiving either.)

Metaphorically, Hart chose to ride his motorbike on the high-speed autobahn of international commerce. He didn't see it as risky because, while a crash might have been catastrophic, he liked the odds of avoiding one.

'I am absolutely anything but a high-risk player. In business terms I am conservative,' he told me. 'The reason people suggest we [at Rank Group] take risks is because they think we carry a lot of debt.'

In his view he's playing a low-risk, predictable game; it just happens to be on an enormous scale. The debt required to get him to that scale may seem risky to you and me, but he considered it a variable over which he has some control. In Hart's world of food and packaging, the market is stable. Prices don't fluctuate much, so it's on you to control your cashflow by running a tight ship and always keeping costs below revenue.

Hart and his team are famously ruthless when it comes to cost control. Within four weeks of taking over Goodman Fielder, he had cut the company's costs by nearly $30 million. The head of almost every key division had been replaced, and Hart had closed the 500-person head office, instead running the multinational business from Burns Philp's 23-person headquarters. 'From a shareholder point of view,' he told me, 'if you've got an agenda that's about improving your business, then every day you waste you leave money on the table.'

In Hart's 'tight ship' model, the stability of his business sectors means lower profit margins (compared to higher-risk, higher-growth businesses), so he leverages up his deals for scale. That allows him to play at the global level and to generate large nominal returns. The only really big variable he has is debt financing, or what we'd think of as interest rates rising and falling. There are times — as with the Burns Philp purchase in 1997 — that he has run close to trouble with that.

But while there are variables around where interest rates might go, they are broadly predictable: you can factor in best- and worst-case scenarios and plan for them. It's a risk that former US defense secretary Donald Rumsfeld might call a known unknown.

Rumsfeld's quadrant

I love the infamous 'Rumsfeld quadrant'. It is a weird piece of American political pop culture, and also quite useful. At a 2002 press conference, answering a question about Iraq and the risks around weapons of mass destruction, the tough Republican politician tied himself up in knots talking about the 'known knowns', 'known unknowns' and 'unknown unknowns'.

Rumsfeld was widely mocked. But putting aside the controversy of the topic itself, what he was trying to say was surprisingly smart. He wasn't making it up, either, but referring to a key piece of US military strategy based on the Johari window, a decision-making philosophy created by cognitive psychologists Joseph Luft and Harrington Ingham in 1955. Let's see if I can do a better job of explaining it than Mr Rumsfeld.

Risk can be divided into four categories which relate to our available information and our understanding of its relevance. These are known knowns, known unknowns, unknown knowns and unknown unknowns.

The most common risks in our life are *known unknowns*. We can be aware that something is a risk, yet lack the relevant data to deal with it. We know the risk is there, but its scale and timing are still unknown. That's how to look at something like borrowing costs. Interest rates are going to move around, and they might even spike. We know that is a risk. What we don't know is exactly when they'll rise or by how much.

	KNOWNS	UNKNOWNS
KNOWNS	**KNOWN KNOWNS** Things we are aware of and understand	**KNOWN UNKNOWNS** Things we are aware of but don't understand
UNKNOWNS	**UNKNOWN KNOWNS** Things we understand but are not aware of	**UNKNOWN UNKNOWNS** Things we are not aware of nor understand

It is also possible to possess highly valuable information but be blissfully unaware that it is relevant to our problem; this is an *unknown known*, and it can be particularly frustrating in hindsight. For example, within an organisation there may be someone who has recognised a problem, but a structural issue may be preventing the information getting to the right people. Usually that structural issue is fear of telling the boss. That happened in the GFC within some of the banks that failed. Some staff had twigged that the complex derivatives they were stacking up on the balance sheet were presenting a huge risk. But they were unable or unwilling to impress that knowledge on those who were powerful enough to deal with the risk.

If we have the information we need and we also know it is relevant, we are fortunate to be dealing with a *known known*. We can see the problem and we are aware of what needs doing to address it. Of course, there is still some risk. When your empty fuel tank light comes on, you know you must get to a petrol station — so if you decide to nip out for one last errand and end up on the side of the motorway, that's on you.

If, however, your fuel tank is full, and you end up stuck on the motorway because environmental activists ran a surprise protest that day, that is an *unknown unknown*. You had no expectation or forewarning of this risk, and you also had no sense of its scale, and so were unprepared for it. Unknown unknowns are the events that come out of the blue. We need to be prepared for life to throw them at us. The best we can do is have broad coping strategies for dealing with sudden change. The Covid-19 pandemic probably falls into this category for most people (although some grumpy epidemiologists would argue that it should have been a known unknown).

What's the point of all these categories? Well, ultimately, awareness about the limits of our knowledge gives us an edge in risk assessment. If we think deeper about what could go wrong, and ask enough questions, we can turn unknown unknowns into known unknowns, says *Risk Intelligence* author Dylan Evans. From there, we can start to seek the specific information we need and ultimately deal more safely and efficiently with risks that are known knowns. We can worry less for better results.

Unfortunately, most humans (billionaires aside) are not great at assessing risk. Animals assess risk innately, whereas we tend to let our theories and biases cloud the logic. Research has proved it. In his 2008 book *The Drunkard's Walk: How Randomness Rules our Lives*, physicist Leonard Mlodinow writes about an experiment that pitted humans against rats as a test of our ability to forecast the odds of things.

This test involved setting up a light to randomly flash either red or green. The subjects (rats and humans) were rewarded for predicting the next colour in the sequence. Overall, the green light was set to flash 75 per cent of the time. The rats quickly worked this out and started picking green every time – ensuring a 75 per cent success rate and plenty of sugary treats. The humans, embarrassingly, had a success rate of about 60 per cent; with their vastly larger brains, they kept trying to see sequencing patterns that simply didn't exist. Pigeons, too, have been shown to outperform humans in experiments that involve assessing odds.

The first step in improving your risk assessment is recognising your bias, and the next is to build strategies to address it. The finance sector has built whole industries and specialist markets to manage risk.

A DERIVATIVE DIVERSION: HOW THE FUTURES MARKET MANAGES RISK

Futures and derivatives offer a specific way to gamble on what the price of something will be at a future date. They can be wildly speculative investments, but they are designed to minimise risk.

Good investors try to minimise risk by diversifying their investments. While big economic cycles often drag all asset classes down, it's rare that every sector collapses at once. So professional investors look to a variety of options, such as cash (a bank account), stocks, bonds, property and commodities.

We talked about bonds earlier, and we touched on the complexity of the secondary market for those bonds. Futures are another kind of secondary market — one that can get even more complex. They are a kind of derivative product, in the sense that what is being sold is a product that derives from another, more basic product. By putting a price on the risk of trading the primary product (and turning that into a product in its own right), markets can effectively buy and sell risk. That allows investors to find a position that suits their risk appetite and, in theory, have some control over likely losses and gains.

Derivatives trading started with commodities, although they can now be sold on all sorts of things — including the mortgage-backed securities that caused the Global Financial Crisis in 2008. The largest and most famous commodities exchange is in Chicago, where future prices for pork bellies, orange juice and all sorts of agricultural products have been bought and sold since the nineteenth century. But the idea of buying and selling goods for delivery at a future date is recorded as far back as ancient Mesopotamia. There are examples all the way through the history of markets.

Futures contracts allow traders to hedge (or insure) their positions against potential losses. For example, farmers can use futures contracts to lock in a price for their crop before harvest to protect against price fluctuations. Essentially, these trades can provide a kind of insurance. Of course, the farmers might lose on the futures contract if the primary commodity price has risen when it comes time to deliver the goods. But they get the security of a guaranteed price, and will get a solid return even if the market price plunges by harvest time.

Big companies also use futures to ensure stable costs for their energy or foreign currency needs. To provide that stability, there are highly specialised investors who are prepared to take the higher risks in order to offer that future price security to those who want it. So, ironically, even though they are designed to trade and distribute risk, futures markets often appear highly volatile and generally aren't something mainstream investors get involved in.

There are variations on futures contracts — such as options, which price in the right to buy or sell but not as an obligation. That means you can pay a premium for a futures contract that you don't need to fulfil if the price moves too far in the wrong direction for you.

Where it starts to get complicated is when people start selling derivatives of derivatives. That's where the notorious structured derivatives that caused the GFC come into play.

Effectively, traders were buying and selling the risk that one party would default on a transaction; but the complexity of the derivatives made assessing that risk increasingly difficult. And in hindsight, people were fixated on easy returns in a booming market, so they weren't trying hard enough to assess the risk anyway. The derivatives market had become dangerously detached from its original function. Unfortunately for the global financial system, some of the world's biggest banks had allowed themselves to be sucked into a speculative bubble chasing big returns.

Graeme Hart was a master at hedging his bets. He steered clear of public stock markets as soon as he'd amassed enough capital to fund his own growth with debt, relying only on his direct relationship with banks. And, as noted above, he was careful to avoid speculative investments in volatile sectors like property, which is what sunk many listed investment firms in the 1987 crash.

The property market can turn sharply, leaving investors badly exposed if interest rates spike at the same time. Prices are often underpinned by confidence that they'll keep rising. If something changes to pop that bubble of confidence, they can plunge, exposing those who have too much debt and not enough cash. That's what happened when the GFC collided with a badly managed and badly regulated non-bank lending finance sector between 2006 and 2010, with consequences that were devastating for many New Zealanders.

Chapter 17

Finance failure: How risk was mis-sold to Kiwis

If you owe the bank $100, that's your problem.
If you owe the bank $100 million,
that's the bank's problem.
— J. Paul Getty

....

n May 2006, National Finance 2000, a small financer of car loans, collapsed owing amateur 'mum and dad' retail investors more than $25 million. Although no one knew it at the time, it was the start of a sorry chapter in New Zealand's investment industry history. In just four years, company collapses dominoed into a monumental meltdown that saw more than 60 companies fail and destroyed some $3 billion of investor saving. The whole thing affected between 150,000 and 200,000 depositors.

What were amateur retail investors doing financing risky car loans for National Finance 2000? In short, they were chasing better interest rate returns than the major banks could offer on traditional savings accounts. Sometimes it was just a couple of per cent more than the bank rate. The catch was that putting your money in a finance company was far riskier than putting it into a bank. People just didn't understand how much riskier.

At the heart of the sector's meltdown was a misunderstanding and misrepresentation of risk. How much should people have been worrying about their investments? A lot more than the finance companies were letting on, as it turned out. The finance companies built marketing strategies that made them appear conservative and sensible, whereas in fact they were taking high risks investing in the speculative end of the property market.

In hindsight, the rates of return on offer, relative to bank rates, should have been a reasonable clue. But hindsight is a fine thing, and in some cases the level of risk was criminally concealed. Even when laws weren't broken, inadequate market regulation meant that the actual nature of the investments and the risks was often buried deep in the fine print of the prospectus documents.

Ironically, the doomed finance company boom had its roots in Kiwis' worries about investing in stock markets after the 1987 crash. Still feeling burned by shares, people were looking for somewhere to invest that was better than a bank account but appeared safer than the stock markets. Finance companies — sometimes described as non-bank lenders — offered to fill that gap. The sector grew through the 1990s, and really took off after 2000. According to Reserve Bank figures, just $10 billion or five per cent of total savings deposits were with non-bank lenders in December 2000. By the end of 2006, as Brian Gaynor pointed out at the time, individual Kiwi investors had $84 billion in deposit-taking organisations (including banks), of which $12 billion, or 15 per cent, was in non-banks, mainly finance companies.

Again, with the beauty of hindsight, there were warnings. A week before National Finance 2000 went into receivership, accounting firm KPMG warned of a growing risk and possible failures shake-out in the finance lending industry in its annual survey of financial institutions.

KPMG said the slowing economy and slowing property market was likely to lead to loan defaults, with new entrants at the greatest risk.

In the immediate aftermath, rating agency Standard & Poor's said the failure showed that 'parts of New Zealand's non-bank financial institutions sector exhibit high risk'.

S&P even highlighted the difficulty investors faced in identifying that risk. But failures at the lower end of the market, such as National Finance 2000, were not an indicator of wider problems for the sector, the Reserve Bank said in its six-monthly Financial Stability Report a few days later. To be fair, the RBNZ did warn that more severe problems for finance companies with property market exposure might emerge further down the track. But the Reserve Bank is always worrying about debt and property investment — so no one listened.

The property market and economy got a second wind and boomed into 2007. As the economy heated up, interest rates soared. The Reserve Bank hiked the Official Cash Rate throughout the year (it peaked at 8.25 per cent in early 2008) but it seemed to have little effect on local investor confidence. What it did do is force finance companies to offer even higher rates to attract investors and then to take even more risk. But the property sector was booming, so the companies were emboldened to keep buying assets, and to keep taking depositors' money to fund those purchases.

The trickle of finance company failures turned into a stream through 2007. Fears grew. The story made the leap from business pages to the TV news with the failure of Bridgecorp in July 2007. Led by controversial figure Rod Petricevic — who'd already had an investment firm fail in the 1987 crash — Bridgecorp collapsed owing 14,500 investors $490 million. In 2012, Petricevic and his fellow directors were convicted of issuing an investment prospectus containing false and misleading statements. He was sentenced to six and a half years in jail.

It's reasonable to wonder if the media could have done a better job of warning investors earlier. We certainly learned a lot. But the law wasn't on our side and the regulation was loose. Trying to report on the risks around these companies and the trouble they were getting into was painfully difficult. We were hampered on almost every story by aggressive legal tactics.

Finance company bosses would argue that newspaper claims that a company was in trouble were spreading panic and making failure even more likely. They pleaded, then they bullied. They would send legal letters, knowing that we had limited budget to respond in kind. I spent many hours working with the *Herald*'s lawyers just to get subtle and often coded warnings into stories. At times, we were forced to run apologies and corrections, which were particularly galling when we knew what was really happening.

But with a full-scale financial meltdown in the US and Europe toppling some of the world's biggest banks in 2008, economic confidence evaporated. The retail banks virtually stopped lending. Asset values plunged, leaving finance companies exposed with dangerously high debts and not enough cash on hand to cover the deposits they'd taken from investors. The trickle of failures became a torrent. All bets were off.

I remember having coffee with a well-connected fund manager who leaned over and whispered in my ear, 'They are all going to go, Liam.' That seemed too shocking to believe. The largest firms, like Hanover and South Canterbury Finance, just seemed too big to fail. Glossy brochures full of impressive numbers, reassuring words and imagery presented a picture of security and stability.

Hanover Finance, owned by Mark Hotchin and businessman Eric Watson, was forced to freeze NZ$554 million owed to 36,500 investors in July 2008. The company had employed popular and trusted TVNZ newsreader Richard Long to front its advertising campaigns. It sponsored the weather forecast on the six o'clock news with the slogan, 'This One Weather update is brought to you by Hanover, a New Zealand business with the size and strength to withstand any conditions.'

It didn't withstand them. The company, with investor deposits still frozen, was sold to Allied Farmers in 2009, giving Hotchin and Watson a clean break. In August, Allied Farmers put their finance company, Allied Nationwide, into receivership.

South Canterbury Finance's fall was even more shocking. It was the largest non-bank lender in the country. Founded in 1926 and owned by conservative Timaru rich-lister Allan Hubbard, it was supposed to be the boring investor in the agricultural sector, but it got well and truly caught up in the speculative end of the 2000s property boom.

At its peak, South Canterbury had 35,000 investors and its assets were estimated to be worth almost NZ$2 billion. After it fell into the hands of receivers in August 2010, investors were shocked to learn they'd been funding trendy bars and nightclubs on Auckland's waterfront. The amount of money involved in that was relatively small — $1.5 million — but it became emblematic of how far South Canterbury had strayed from core business.

It suffered much bigger losses on tourist resorts and upmarket property developments in Wānaka and Queenstown. Such was the level of trust in Hubbard and South Canterbury, however, that investors kept coming even after the big meltdowns of the GFC in 2008.

What happened? Had the elderly Hubbard been led astray? Or was he reckless or greedy, or just naïve? We'd never get the full story; he died in a car crash in 2011 while still facing 50 charges of serious fraud.

Taxpayer bailout and wider cost

In the end, some of the biggest losers in the finance company collapse did get kind of lucky. With fears the GFC might threaten Australasian banks — or at least cause a dangerous loss of confidence in them — both the Australian and New Zealand governments hurriedly put taxpayer-backed deposit guarantees in place in October 2008.

The New Zealand government included finance company deposits (for firms where assets weren't yet frozen), providing a lifeline to the likes of South Canterbury investors — but eventually costing taxpayers $2 billion.

'I was not keen on guaranteeing the finance companies,' former minister of finance Sir Michael Cullen told me in 2018. Cullen said he'd been working with the Reserve Bank on a more measured guarantee scheme — one that could have avoided bailing out the likes of South Canterbury. He said he was well aware of the moral hazard associated with providing state support for high-risk investments.

But one Sunday afternoon in October 2008, just as Prime Minister Helen Clark was about to go on stage and launch Labour's election campaign, they got word that Australia was announcing its own deposit guarantee that day. 'As we were preparing for Helen's speech ... basically in the green room at the Town Hall ... word came through from Canberra of rumours that Kevin Rudd was about to make a major announcement,' Cullen recalled.

Rudd, seemingly acting unilaterally, had put New Zealand in an impossible position. 'At that point we were very worried that if the Aussies did that and we did nothing, there would be a loud sucking sound of capital going from New Zealand to Australia,' Cullen said.

They couldn't afford to wait for markets to open on Monday, and carving out the major non-banks was too complex to do in a hurry. Because they were so close to the election, Cullen ran the idea past National's Bill English and he agreed. 'I don't know where [Rudd] got his advice from,' Cullen told me. 'The Australian banks, and therefore fundamentally the New Zealand banks, were sound because they just hadn't gotten into all those complex derivatives.'

For Cullen, who died in 2021, the cost to taxpayers of the deposit guarantee scheme was a source of some regret. In my opinion he was a great finance minister. And unlike the entrepreneurs I've met over the years, he hated risk and did not like to take chances with money. 'I've been a very conservative saver. I've never ventured outside the bank,' he told me in a late interview. 'Money in itself is not a goal in life,' he said.

In fact, New Zealand has been well served by fiscally conservative finance ministers over the years. Those I've had most to do with — Cullen, Bill English and Grant Robertson — have all had a distinctly cautious approach to money in their own personal lives. Cullen's only obvious indulgence was a Jaguar sports car, to improve the comfort of his daily commute. 'In the end, what a degree of affluence gives is choices in life,' Cullen said. That seems like a good outlook for any politician seeking to lift the wealth of average Kiwis.

A capital killer

Aside from the taxpayer bailout and ripped-off investors, there was one more sorry economic flow-on from the finance company crashes. They effectively killed the second-tier 'non-bank lending' market for at least a decade. That's a shame, because riskier lending shouldn't be inherently bad.

Kiwi investors piled back into residential property investment with a vengeance through the 2010s. They also came around to safer balanced share market investments via KiwiSaver — a much more memorable legacy of Michael Cullen's political career. KiwiSaver keeps risk levels simple and easy to understand, breaking them down into categories like conservative, moderate, balanced and growth.

So, New Zealanders are starting to get better at judging financial risk. But we want those people with the spare capital and higher appetite for risk (and higher returns) to have a go. If capital is directed to useful sectors, such as technology and biotechnology, it helps grow the economy in the longer term. Without that kind of higher-risk investing, a country won't be as productive as it could be.

Angel investing, venture capital markets, second-tier finance company lenders and even equity markets are all there for people with varied degrees of risk appetite. They help drive technological progress, solve environmental problems and even fund great music and movies. The issue is around the open and accurate disclosure of risks and likely returns. That stuff needs to be aligned with investor expectations from the start.

Clearly finance company investors in New Zealand were up against a lack of information, which was either poorly presented or in some cases criminally concealed. (For the record, National Finance 2000 boss Trevor Allan Ludlow was sentenced to nearly six years in jail for theft. His fellow directors were also prosecuted.) But in many cases, there was also a serious lack of investor knowledge about the relevant questions that needed to be asked. That's what makes the losses so painful to investors, many of them elderly, who poured their retirement savings into finance company debentures in the 2000s.

Put it this way: if you sprain your ankle doing the Coast to Coast event, you're not going to feel as frustrated as you would if you did the damage getting up off the couch. If you lose $100,000 gambling at a casino, you kind of knew you were being reckless. If you lose $100,000 from what you thought was a bank savings account, you'll feel cheated.

THE SUNK COST FALLACY AND THE DANGER OF EMOTIONS

There are plenty of economic terms that are just fancy words for things we already say. Everyone knows what it means to 'cut your losses'. On that basis, it shouldn't be hard to understand the idea of sunk costs and the sunk cost fallacy. It's basically not cutting your losses when you ought to.

A sunk cost is simply a cost that has already been incurred and can't be recovered. When it comes to rational economic decision-making, those costs are no longer relevant. They're gone. We can all understand that, but most of us are guilty of falling for the sunk cost fallacy. That's because we allow ourselves to get emotionally invested in things, and then we factor sunk costs into our decision-making. The more emotionally invested we are, the harder it is to cut our losses, even though the consequence of not cutting them might result in a worse overall outcome.

In the financial world, the sunk cost fallacy is something good investors strive to avoid. Say an investor buys a stock at $1 a share. If those shares fall by 25 per cent, a bad investor might hold on, hoping the shares will make a comeback so they can avoid realising their loss. But why wait for those shares to rebound? If there's another investment opportunity that looks better, then it is time to cut your losses and move on.

Many traders lock in hard-and-fast rules about losses: they might decide to always sell and move on if a share price falls 10 or 15 per cent. In the professional investment world, there is no room for sentiment and emotion. The notion of opportunity cost (see page 35) should always be front and centre of decision-making. Money that isn't making money is wasted money.

But in the real world, we fall for the sunk cost fallacy all the time. When we watch a bad movie right to the end, we're wasting time that might be better spent on something more fun. People stay in a toxic relationship because they convince themselves they've invested too much time to give up on it.

Business and governments make bad decisions and get bad results when they start to put too much weight on sunk costs. One of the most famous examples of this is the Concorde fallacy. In the 1960s, the French and British governments launched a joint programme to build a supersonic jet airliner.

Over a decade of development, the costs blew out by more than 30 times the original estimates.

They forged on, even though it was obvious those costs meant the plane would never be economically worthwhile to commercially produce and run.

Chapter 18

What do I know? Fireside words of financial wisdom

A wise person should have money in their head,
but not in their heart.
— Jonathan Swift

....

Let's bring it back to that key BBQ question. How worried should we be about our investments? Or the economy? How worried should we be about a recession or losing our job? What — to cut to the chase — is the real secret to being good with money?

I've talked with some of the smartest financial and economic thinkers in New Zealand and the world. I've talked with the top economists and stockbrokers and bankers. I've talked with the chief executives, the board chairs, the entrepreneurs and the venture capitalists. I've learned an awful lot about money and how to make it. In fact, I've learned so much that I sometimes think I've had to go out of my way to avoid getting rich.

Here's a shameful example. Sometime around 2006, shortly before he launched his cloud-based accounting software company Xero, tech sector entrepreneur Rod Drury took me out to lunch and explained his whole plan. Drury had already had success building two tech start-ups and selling them for several million dollars. But he was looking for investment money to move fast, and on a much more ambitious scale, with Xero. From me I guess he was looking for publicity and positive local media coverage.

I really liked Drury. He was a surfer and we spoke much the same language; he convinced me to get back into skateboarding, tweeting advice on the best kind of longboard for a middle-aged skater. His lunchtime pitch was utterly compelling. I was convinced that he had the right product, the right strategy and the right kind of drive and energy to create a world-class tech company.

On that basis I was happy to be an early champion of Xero as a Kiwi success story. But I never invested — even though, during that lunch, I was offered the chance to get in before the company went public. Less than a year later, Xero listed on the New Zealand stock exchange for $1 a share, giving the company a value of $55 million. Xero is now listed on the Australian stock exchange with a market value of around $20 billion.

It's hard to be exact about the maths because it's all hypothetical, but it's safe to say that if I had rustled up 10 grand to throw in with Drury at that early pre-float stage, it would be worth a few million now. Yikes!

There are other examples of companies where I've seen the turnaround story, there are property cycles I've seen come and go, and there's the rise of cryptocurrency. I first wrote about the (then) crazy new Bitcoin thing in April 2013 because the technology seemed weird and interesting. It was creating an investment buzz, having just soared in value to more than US$100. In late 2023, one Bitcoin was worth about US$30,000, having been up as high as US$65,000! Would I have held on and sold at the peak? Who knows? I didn't buy any and have never been tempted.

But if you write about money and you aren't rich, you kind of have to ask why. Am I just stupid? Or lazy? Or too risk-averse? Possibly the latter. But I also lack a passion for managing my money in a way that makes more money. A lot of what's involved is administration, filling out forms and so on. I don't care enough to put the effort in where it's required to maximise the investment potential of every excess dollar I have. Rather, my ambition has been to write and be a journalist — and money famously isn't a massive by-product of the profession.

Funnily enough, though, the more I've talked with successful business-people, the more I've found that they are not so different. None of the wealthy people I've interviewed has ever told me they chased money as an end in itself; it has always been a by-product of what they love doing. 'I don't equate it with being a better person . . . I don't believe that whoever dies the richest has won,' Theresa Gattung told me on the *Money Talks* podcast in 2021. 'Money for me is totally about freedom.'

Gattung became the first female chief executive of a major publicly listed company at just 37 when she took the top job at Telecom in 1999. These days she is a company director, entrepreneur, philanthropist and investor.

'I believe that money is an energy: if you both spend and give, you will get back,' Gattung said. 'This sounds a bit airy-fairy, I know. But I thought that I've got to keep that energy flowing. I've never thought it was my own individual brilliance, I've always seen it as a co-creation. It's sometimes just sheer good luck.'

But both investing and being a successful entrepreneur do take a certain attitude. It's not just about being smart and in the right place at the right time. 'It's about being prepared to take risks,' Gattung told me. 'If you don't have that genie in you, if that's not part of your DNA make-up, that's fine; stay in the corporate world, don't become an entrepreneur.'

As she suggests, if you're going to make it as an entrepreneur you've got to know how to do a deal.

The power of holding your tongue

Some people, like Graeme Hart, seem to have been born with an extra gene for picking when to buy, when to sell and when to walk away. But if it doesn't come naturally, don't worry. Sir Owen Glenn, who has done his fair share of big deals over the past 40 years, says it is a knack that can be learned. 'There is a lot of personality in it,' he told me in 2010. 'But it comes through experience.'

Glenn reckoned there was a lot to be said for not saying a lot. 'I believe the essence of negotiation is not what you say. It is the periods of silence. You say what you have to say and then say nothing,' he said. 'Let the other guy work out how he's going to answer you. I find that works. Don't try and be cute about it. A lot of people will make their point, then follow that up with unnecessary statements to say how right they are. Just say it, then let them comment. Because that tells you everything.'

Sir Owen probably would have been a good journalist, because that's also decent advice for the art of interviewing. Glenn is a character. A charismatic rogue, a philanthropist, and the toughest businessman I ever interviewed. You don't make the thick end of a billion dollars running a logistics business out of Monaco without being a hard man.

In 2018, I asked Glenn how he looked at money at that point and he was dismissive (despite the fact we were sitting on his superyacht at the time). 'I have to take a very quick look,' he says. 'It doesn't last long in my hands.' In fact, he said he doesn't really handle money much these days. 'It's a commodity. It's just like keeping the books — income and expenditure.'

Glenn has been generous with his wealth in this country, financing the Auckland Business School and NZ Hockey among many other things. He has that philanthropic streak in common with another famous self-made Kiwi, Stephen Tindall.

The mild-mannered Tindall, who founded The Warehouse in 1982, seems to be profoundly normal in a way that is unusual for someone who has been so successful and surrounded by wealth for so long. 'My parents were not that well off,' he told me during an interview in 2010. 'They taught us to be frugal. So, I was really into saving.'

Tindall's first jobs were mowing lawns and then delivering groceries on a bike. 'When I turned 15, I got my licence and delivered them with a truck. I was always doing odd jobs and earning pocket money from my parents, worked holiday jobs with my dad,' he said. 'I watched my father, who was quite entrepreneurial and who made things at home and sold them to retail stores, and my mother had her own hairdressing business at home as well. So, I was kind of brought up by a couple of entrepreneurial parents.'

Tindall is intensely patriotic. He literally flies the flag for New Zealand in his modest Auckland office. He's also unashamedly positive. 'Can anybody tell us a better place?' he asked. 'We might not be the wealthiest, but we care about each other. I think there is so much more we can do to help with inequality and environment . . . with getting everyday New Zealanders involved in tech businesses — whether they're running them or investing in them.

'I'm incredibly optimistic,' he told me. 'I just wish I was 30 again.'

THE ORACLE OF OMAHA

Optimism is, without a doubt, a key attribute of successful businesspeople. An economist can always find something to worry about. The trick is to somehow take those risks on board without allowing them to deter you from acting. Pessimism is no way to create wealth. You have to back yourself. But realism is important.

US billionaire (and relentless optimist) Warren Buffett once told me: 'Recognise what you can't do. Only swing at what's in the strike zone.' Okay, it wasn't exactly a one-on-one chat. In 2016 I was one of almost 40,000 fans who packed a stadium in Omaha, Nebraska, to hear the so-called Oracle of Omaha speak at his investment firm Berkshire Hathaway's annual general meeting.

It's a pilgrimage for investors from all over the world — one that I got to make by tagging along with Pie Funds founder Mike Taylor. The then 85-year-old Buffett and his 92-year-old sidekick and business partner Charlie Munger spent five hours sharing their folksy personal philosophy on business, economics, investing and life in general.

There's obviously no shortage of Buffett investment advice in the world. His top tips are to start early, be patient and back the power of the stock market to create wealth over time. He doesn't recommend individual stock picking for most people, advising them to track the wider market with managed funds. But if you do decide to have a go — as he did — you should look for value. In his 2008 letter to shareholders, he wrote:

'Price is what you pay; value is what you get. Whether we're talking about socks or stocks, I like buying quality merchandise when it is marked down.'

Buffet also claims he's had good luck, too; but when I heard him speak, he did admit to having something of a knack for 'pattern recognition'. He is fascinated by the world of micro-economics (i.e. affecting individuals, households and firms), but isn't much interested in macro-economics — laughing when asked what he thinks will happen to the price of oil.

Munger, who was still giving fascinating media interviews in 2023 at nearly 100 years old — was even more direct. 'Micro-economics is business,' he says. 'Macro-economics is what you put up with.' That's not a reason to ignore the bigger picture. Buffett advises people to stay interested in all aspects of money and to never stop learning.

One quote that stuck with me was his advice for surviving recessions and other hard times. 'The best thing you can do is to be exceptionally good at something. Whatever abilities you have can't be taken away from you . . . The best investment by far is anything that develops yourself, and it's not taxed at all.'

Invest in yourself: you can't lose even if you don't get rich. It's great advice.

A Wheeler and a dealer

Money advice doesn't necessarily have to be straightforward stuff like studying hard or understanding compound interest. It might just be travelling and getting experience in the world.

I got that kind of advice from one of the smartest economic thinkers I've had the privilege of talking to, former Reserve Bank governor Graeme Wheeler. I did several long interviews with Wheeler during his tenure as governor from 2012 to 2017.

A handy all-round cricketer (who briefly represented his home province of Wellington), Wheeler worked his way through positions at the Treasury, but really made his mark at the World Bank in Washington DC, where for four years he was managing director of operations, overseeing 12,000 staff and a US$1.7 billion budget. Wheeler developed a deep understanding of how the global monetary system works. A lot of his politically balanced economic thinking informs the tone throughout this book.

But he told me once that it was his experiences *without* money that really taught him about it. 'One of the best things I ever did in life was, twice in my twenties, I took off travelling around the world. I did it deliberately to experience a different side of life and try to understand hardship, disadvantage and discrimination,' he said. 'You're essentially living on your wits, sleeping on streets, living with almost no money.'

It obviously fed a passion to dedicate himself to economics. The Wellington rumour mill had it that Wheeler didn't get on well with the prime minister of the day, John Key, who supposedly had some different views on monetary policy direction at certain points in their professional relationship.

Like Wheeler, Key is also extremely savvy with money. He comes from the dealing room – he's a currency trader who made his mark in one of the toughest business environments there is. He has the instincts of a great gambler and once told me he might have made a career in the horse-racing industry if his mother had let him. Ruth Key, a solo mum, worried about his financial future and pushed him towards the more secure path of an accounting degree. But before long, the young Key opted instead for a job handling foreign exchange for Elders Finance in Wellington. He thrived.

There is a fantastic video clip, still available online, from a 1987 episode of current affairs show *Close Up*. The piece looks behind the scenes at the allegedly glamorous world of currency trading. It pulls out all the stops to present dealing rooms of the day as action-packed Wall Street-style dens of testosterone. Star of the show is the young John Key, who is more than happy to play along with the premise. The reporter boldly declares that

Key 'relishes making decisions almost faster than the speed of conscious thought'. That's something his critics have probably always suspected.

More revealing is an interview with Key's boss at the time, Chris Wright, then a manager at Elders Finance. Asked what makes Key so good, he replied: 'John has an uncanny ability to know when to hold positions and when to cut positions.'

That's it. That is what made Key good as a trader, and it's also an uncanny description of what made him so successful as a politician. Before that, he had worked his way up to be global head of foreign exchange for US investment bank Merrill Lynch. I once asked Key whether currency trading was an art or a science, and he was emphatic that it is the former. Research and strategy are good things to have done. They'll inform your intuition. If you don't do your economic homework, you will be at a disadvantage. But in something like currency trading, the decision-making happens so fast that great intuition is needed. There's no time for second-guessing yourself.

Key is now a company director and board chair. He has the big roles — like chair of ANZ New Zealand — but also picks smaller start-up firms to get involved with. When I interviewed him in 2022, he told me the best piece of financial advice he was ever given was to live within your means. (He also told me he'd just bought a helicopter.)

When I asked him for his best financial advice for young Kiwis, he was very direct: understand the power of compound interest and buy property. 'I know people will say that's a very hard thing to do if you don't have a deposit and you don't have the bank of Mum and Dad, I get all that stuff,' he said. He's also aware that it's controversial advice given the perennial debate about house prices. But it works, and it is a reliable path for those looking to get ahead, in his mind. 'And it's not because I think it's so tax-advantageous, even though there are some tax advantages. It makes you save. You pay off some principal and some interest on your loan; if you have some spare cash or a bonus or something you pay off some more.'

Having grown up without much of the folding stuff, Key acknowledges that 'money really matters — nothing terrifies people more than that they'll run out of money and have no money to retire on'. But if he were a slave to money, he would never have dropped out of the finance sector to spend 15 years as a politician, he said. 'Initially, working is about money and putting food on the table, but the reality is there are so many other things that come out of that. It's that connectivity.'

You'd almost think he was a lefty with that kind of talk![19]

Choice (bro)

In the end, the goal of financial success is mostly about seeking more choice in how we live our lives. Helping more Kiwis achieve that goal was one of the motivations for Leighton Roberts, who co-founded popular stock market trading app Sharesies.

Roberts told me the social inequality he saw in the investment world was one of his driving reasons for creating Sharesies. 'The fundamental problem is that people don't start on an equal footing, right? Most New Zealanders get their financial advice from their parents, or someone close.' And, he adds, too few Kiwis have good role models when it comes to money.

Lack of education, low wages or issues like a lingering fear of the stock market (after the wipe-out New Zealanders endured in 1987) pushed people away from direct investment, he said. 'So, we have a huge amount of people, and a huge amount of our economy, involved in housing as opposed to productive companies. The economics are a little bit twisted in New Zealand. I do think places are happier when there's much more equality. That's not to say I don't think you need more wealthy people as well. But that's not an ambition in itself. It's a by-product of something that you've achieved.'

There we go with that by-product again!

Roberts was a trumpet player in the New Zealand Army band until real life intervened and he found himself working at Kiwibank. But he'd always

---

19   He definitely isn't.

had a personal interest in investing. At Kiwibank he and some co-workers had a good idea for making it easier to do, and they realised that between them they had the skills to execute that idea. He and five mates started Sharesies in 2017 with just $20,000. 'When you've got six people trying to live off of it and build a company on it, it's not a whole lot of money.'

The trading app has gone on to transform New Zealand's investing landscape — particularly for younger people — allowing investors to buy into the share market with as little as $5. As of 2023, Sharesies has signed up more than half a million investors and has $2 billion of funds under management. That's pretty big money until you consider what mainstream banking looks like.

New Zealand's largest bank, ANZ New Zealand, looks after nearly $140 billion in deposits, it manages $34 billion in investment funds and made a profit of about $2.3 billion in 2022. That same year, ANZ NZ's chief executive Antonia Watson also told me that, despite working in finance, she had never chased money as a goal in itself. 'Money is an enabler to other parts of your life,' she said. 'It's not the be-all and end-all, but I think I had an early appreciation of the value of money — those little things like taking the coins to the bank and knowing that was now sitting in a savings book.'

Watson described herself as 'a lazy investor'. In other words, she just follows the basic rules of personal finance. 'I tend to get someone else to do the work for me,' she said. 'Most of our money is in managed funds, on the more growth [end] of the scale.

'Pay off your home, save for a rainy day, manage for the risk. There is still a lack of financial literacy in New Zealand,' she said. The best piece of advice Watson ever got on money — possibly from her mother — was simply 'the miracle of compound interest . . . Money does make money, even if it's as simple as a term deposit.'

That's basically what Key said, too. It's what Buffett said and what any other credible voice on personal finance will tell you. Understand the exponential power of compound interest — both as a savings tool and as a warning for the kind of trap debt can be.

You and your money

You should listen to experts and consider their advice. You should pay attention to the economy around you. But the experts don't know what makes you happy. They haven't framed their work to address your personal doubts and worries. Their information and analysis become more useful if we turn these questions inwards and put them in the context of our own risk appetite.

We all need to think more about the psychology of risk. We should talk about it in schools from an early age. It should go hand in hand with the maths we learn about probability. Let's recognise we are bad at risk assessment and, in doing so, get better at it.

If you really understand how much worry you can handle, and if you build your financial and economic decisions around that, you're unlikely to go too far wrong. By all means push yourself, step out into the deeper water — take a risk! If you want to get wealthy, you'll probably need to. Actually, to succeed at most things in life, you'll need to take some risk.

But you can't take a meaningful step in the right direction unless you understand where you're standing in the first place. The professionals know that if you have a strategy that fits your personal circumstances and your temperament (or your clients'), it provides some insurance against disappointment. I've heard highly successful investors talk about being sure that your investment strategy passes the 'sleep at night test'. If you are taking so much risk that you can't sleep, something is out of whack.

I reckon life's too short to spend it worrying all the time. Make sure you're worrying about the right things, the things that matter most to you.

Chapter 19

Back to the future: An economic crystal ball

Life can only be understood backwards;
but it must be lived forwards.
— Søren Kierkegaard

....

I t's nice to open a chapter with a quote from an obscure philosopher, even if it is just to remind us that we spend our lives navigating through the rear-view mirror. But picking what is going to happen next is one of the big reasons people pay attention to economics.

These days, it seems we expect our economists to perform like astrologers and tell us what life has in store for us. What future awaits our children? Where will they work and what will they do? Are we headed for a 1950s utopia of flying electric cars and unlimited leisure, or a gritty 1980s-style noir dystopia of threatening AI robots?

Coming down to earth a little, what about our everyday economic worries? Will inflation get worse or better? What does our aging population do to the equations? When push comes to shove, we mostly just want to know what the economy will do later this year — or, more specifically, whether we'll be able to afford an overseas holiday.

IT'S ALL IN THE MIND

Humans are hard-wired to hate uncertainty. Neuroscience suggests we have a bit in our brain called the limbic system that has evolved to react to uncertainty as if it were pain or danger, creating a fight-or-flight response. (The ability to cope with uncertainty has been identified as a valuable leadership trait, which is why science like this limbic system stuff doesn't spend long in a lab these days before someone clever starts teaching it at a business school and it pops up all over LinkedIn.)

Studies have found that people hate uncertainty so much, they will pay a price, or forgo a bargain, to avoid it. Not for nothing do we assert that 'a bird in the hand is worth two in the bush'. In 2006, economists ran an experiment with students which involved trading cash for retail gift cards.[20] They found that people were willing to pay $38 for a $50 gift card, but they were only willing to pay $28 for a lottery ticket that would yield either a $50 or $100 gift card with equal probability. Most preferred to pay more for the certainty of the $50. Irrational as it sounds, the dislike of uncertainty evidently clouds our judgement.

We generally trust economists to future-cast because the work they perform seems like science, with its graphs and maths and experiments. The economists who work for banks and other financial organisations are also subject to ruthless commercial pressure. They're expected to produce monthly or quarterly forecasts for economic trends with very specific numbers attached. They have to place public bets on where unemployment, inflation or GDP will land — down to the decimal point. And the numbers they choose matter, because they might make the difference between forecasting a recession and picking that we skipped one. But can they really predict the future? Well, that depends on how you define 'prediction'.

---

20   John List, Uri Gneezy and George Wu, 'The Uncertainty Effect: When a Risky Prospect Is Valued Less Than Its Worst Possible Outcome', *Quarterly Journal of Economics*, vol. 121, no. 4 (November 2006), 1283–1309, DOI:10.1093/qje/121.4.1283.

Getting it right most of the time

We humans are pretty good at creating predictive models — expectations, modelled on past events, that give odds on what might be coming. But the sheer variability of the world we interact with means things often don't go the way they are supposed to. For that reason, economists also spend a lot of time explaining — in advance — why they could be wrong.

One thing that economists do to give themselves leeway is hedge their bets. It may look like cheating, but they usually pick a range of scenarios — typically a best case, a worst case and a central (or base) case. If you're reading an economic forecast and thinking about what it means for your plans to invest, these scenarios are useful because they set some parameters and provide realistic expectations.

Ultimately, we're looking for economists to get the trend right. Is something going up or down? Is the economy growing or shrinking? On that kind of binary basis, economists are far more accurate — and that is very useful information if you are planning to start a business or buy a house.

It's a bit like meteorology. We expect weather forecasts to warn us broadly if we are in for a sunny or rainy day, but not necessarily predict the exact hour of rainfall. Similarly, studies have shown economic forecasts are pretty good out to about three months, and no better than a guess once we get out past a year.

Everyone knows the saying 'A stopped clock is right twice a day'. There's an economics version of that one: 'Economists have successfully predicted nine of the last five recessions.' Economist Paul Samuelson is often credited with using the line in a 1966 magazine article (although he told it with the stock market as the butt of the joke). The point is that if you take a negative position on the economy and stick with it, you'll be right eventually. Indeed, a long-term study of forecasting published by the IMF in 2018 concluded that recessions aren't that rare, with economies in a state of recession 10–12 per cent of the time.

What *was* rare, the study found, was a recession that was forecast well in advance.[21] Complaints about economic forecasts usually relate to specific calls — how much house prices were supposed to fall, that kind of thing. But it is much less common for events to fall outside the range of scenarios economists have modelled.

In the first weeks and months of the pandemic, almost all the economists got their forecasts wrong because they didn't have a useful historic model to work off. The last time the world had had a pandemic was in 1918, when the world was a completely different place. Economists were flying in the dark, and that quote about life only being understood backwards was never truer.

Despite their flaws, though, I think economic forecasts add to our net balance of certainty. Not by specifically picking the unemployment or GDP numbers, or house prices, but from the context they provide. They help us to see why our interest rates are likely to rise or fall in coming months. They can forewarn of rising unemployment or inflation or other trends that will affect our finances. They provide a framework and give us insight into the patterns that drive change.

The tech gamble

Artificial intelligence, flying drones, space tourism, genetic engineering, cryptocurrency, the wild stream of social media battles and environmental meltdown: it was all there in the science fiction we grew up with. Now it's suddenly all happening. The sense of panic, though, the feeling that it is all accelerating out of control, isn't really new.

Alvin Toffler's popular sociological take on futurism, *Future Shock*, was written back in 1970. The premise of the best-seller was that human brains weren't hard-wired to cope with the increasingly rapid pace of technological change we were inflicting upon ourselves in the modern era.

---

21 Zidong An, João Tovar Jalles and Prakash Loungani, 'How Well Do Economists Forecast Recessions?', IMF Working Paper, 2018, available at www.imf.org/-/media/Files/Publications/WP/2018/wp1839.ashx.

Toffler, weirdly, is immortalised in New Zealand culture, via the lyrics to the song 'Victoria' by the Dance Exponents, with Jordan Luck citing *Cosmopolitan* and Alvin Toffler to illustrate his protagonist's sophisticated taste.

Ironically, Toffler's place in thousands of drunken Kiwi singalongs is a profoundly nostalgic one. But the guy made a very good point about the future, one that has become increasingly relevant as the pace of change has accelerated.

Looking years into the future and guessing where tech will take us is very much a lottery. Take the internet, for instance. It is the biggest technological change of my lifetime, and I definitely didn't see it coming. I remember, as a reporter in the mid-1990s, going with my community newspaper colleagues to the local library for a demonstration of the power of this new internet thing. Yahoo was opened and we were told we could look up anything we wanted. But we couldn't think of anything we needed to look up. The experience was profoundly underwhelming.

The technologists on Wall Street at the time thought otherwise. Over the second half of the 1990s, money poured into internet companies as people who understood how it worked positioned themselves to get rich off it. Most of them didn't get rich — at least, not for another decade or so. The internet investment boom would become known as the dot.com bubble and then as the tech wreck.

Between 1995 and its peak in March 2000, the tech-heavy Nasdaq stock market index skyrocketed. Investors piled into companies that didn't make profits, companies that didn't even have revenue streams, giving them ridiculous values. There was a new internet start-up for every aspect of modern life. Most of them were retailers and media companies, anticipating that we'd soon be doing all our shopping and reading and viewing online. They weren't wrong. They were just too early. The tech wasn't ready, or the world wasn't — or both. The money ran out before the mass adoption of the internet arrived.

The Nasdaq index rose fivefold between 1995 and 2000, but then crashed from a peak of 5048 on 10 March 2000 to just 1140 by October

2002 — a 77 per cent fall. Trillions of dollars of hypothetical value were created and then erased during the boom and bust. Less than a decade later, smartphones and faster internet changed the game, and the predictions about the world-changing power of the internet came true.

A few veterans, such as Amazon and Google, survived, and emerged leaner and stronger to dominate when the public finally caught up. But it took until 2015 for the Nasdaq to surpass that millennial peak.

The tech wreck is an excellent reminder that, even if we can see the path of new technology, we can't necessarily predict when it will hit the mainstream. Even being a few years out can be disastrous for investors.

At the time of writing, many people fear history will repeat in the form of the AI boom, which has grabbed the popular imagination since the launch of the ChatGPT chatbot in late 2022. Companies associated with AI have soared. The California chip-maker Nvidia saw its value rise by 270 per cent in 2023 to give it a market capitalisation of more than US$1 trillion. Will AI deliver the change we all expect and fear? Probably. But for market investors, the question is more acute: will it deliver fast enough to justify the money that's been sunk into it?

Is everything getting worse or better?

Before we speculate on the changes AI is about to unleash upon our world, it may be reassuring to note how a lot of stuff has turned out better than the experts — and we ordinary folk — feared.

With a few optimistic exceptions, I think our expectations of the future and new technology have really been shaped by dystopian visions. Mary Shelley's *Frankenstein*, Aldous Huxley's *Brave New World* and George Orwell's *1984* . . . many of the milestone works of science fiction foretold grim outcomes.

The Population Bomb, a 1968 best-seller by US biologists Paul and Anne Ehrlich, famously predicted global famine and mass starvation across the West by the 1970s–80s. The Ehrlichs, among others, were convinced that the world was approaching its population limit. But the world's population has doubled since 1968, and, while there are plenty of problems for humans to worry about, food production isn't one of them. Where famine still exists, it is primarily a symptom of war and corruption.

The Ehrlichs fell into what economists call the Malthusian trap — named after eighteenth-century economist Thomas Malthus. He applied biology to human economics, noting that successful populations typically start to grow at an exponential rate. Biologists observing wild animal populations saw how that much growth leads to collapse. In the absence of natural predators or disease, populations can quickly exhaust food supply.

The theory holds up well for clams or birds, but not so much for humans. Malthus made two mistakes. First, he underestimated the potential of technology — and food production — to expand exponentially alongside population, a challenge in which we have more than succeeded. (In doing so, we may have super-heated the earth into another potentially apocalyptic scenario — but that is another story.)

A HEATED DEBATE: THE ECONOMICS OF GLOBAL WARMING

Climate change is a problem for economists (and, of course, for everyone else). The big social and economic changes required to mitigate it are under way, and they will be costly. In 2022, consultancy McKinsey estimated the cost of getting the global economy to net zero emissions by 2050 would require about US$275 trillion.

That's pretty expensive. But even if we ignored the human costs of drought and floods and heat, the economic cost of doing nothing would also be terrible. A 2022 report by consultancy Deloitte concludes that, if left unchecked, climate change could cost the global economy US$178 trillion over the next 50 years, or a 7.6 per cent cut to global GDP in the year 2070 alone. Beyond that, it just gets worse.

So, moving rapidly to address the issue should be a no-brainer. Unfortunately, people and politics make it a bit more complex. How do we progress? How do we allocate the burden of the costs? How can we regulate? Do we tax more or offer tax breaks? Should we harness market forces to help send price signals on carbon costs and to drive new technologies?

Essentially, climate change highlights all the ongoing political divisions in economics and adds a time limit on resolving them. How fast can we drive change without destroying our ability to create wealth? If change is too radical and breaks down economic systems, we will have a new set of global problems.

If you're a relatively wealthy business or individual, you can afford to make rational economic choices that will mitigate the effects of climate change, even if they come at a short-term cost. But if you're struggling to feed or house your children, issues like climate change will always be a lower priority. This creates something of a catch-22. We need poor nations to develop enough that their populations can afford to think more about the environment. But the model for that development — for the past 200 years — has involved rapid increases in carbon output.

Clearly it is up to richer nations to lead from the front. We must move at pace to develop and deploy new green technology that will enable us to maintain a standard of living and developing nations to improve theirs. We need to tax carbon polluters. (New Zealand's world-leading Emissions Trading Scheme represents a bold effort to share the burden of the costs via market mechanisms.)

But democracies with short election cycles require politicians to maintain popular support. Policies that involve making people poorer can be a hard sell.

The other mistake Malthus made was assuming human populations would always grow exponentially. It's true that the global population has grown rapidly since the Industrial Revolution. Infant mortality has fallen; life expectancy has grown. But in the past 50–60 years, the emergence of a new technology has changed the game. The contraceptive pill has given women much more control over their own reproductive capacity. In tandem with social progress that has seen much higher rates of education for women, birth rates have been declining in wealthy nations for several decades now.

I'm suspicious of the idea that the world is necessarily getting worse. Were things really that much better in the past — or is it simply that my knees hurt more? We humans tend to have a nostalgia bias, especially as we age, and there is something intuitive about the way we romanticise the past and see the future as bleak. It might come back to the brain's love of certainty.

The lack of control over the future encourages us to catastrophise. And sure, what we're facing on the climate front seems to be unambiguously grim right now. But what if we crack cold fusion? Maybe a game-changing scientific breakthrough will deliver cheap sustainable energy to the world. That might seem hopelessly optimistic, but it happens. Anyone remember the ozone hole?

I'm not really suggesting there is a silver bullet for climate change — but however humans do get through this crisis, you can bet it will involve technology. Perhaps it will take the organisational power of AI to drive the kind of social behavioural changes we'll need to make.

Economists and social scientists have to try to cut through the nostalgia bias, and our fear of tech, when they look at future trends and try to answer the questions that worry us. What, for example, will the latest wave of AI computing do to our economies? Will it create wealth or unemployment? The future of work has become a very popular topic in the business pages for the past decade or so.

Smart computers, stupid humans

AI could be a wonderful new tool for humanity, but like most people right now I'm nervous about the disruption and radical social change it's about to cause. I reckon the problem won't be the smart computers, it will be the stupid humans. It's almost always the same with new technology. From the Tree of Knowledge to the Industrial Revolution, humans always stuff it up.

Take, for instance, Gutenberg's movable-type printing press of the 1450s. What turned out to be about 200 years of religious war began in Europe within 20 years of its invention. The printed word allowed the rapid spread of ideas and played a big role in the emerging Renaissance. Classical works of art and science that had previously been buried in church basements could be copied and widely shared. Clearly, on balance the printing press has added great value to human life. But if you asked a German in the sixteenth or early seventeenth century, with the country locked in almost perpetual religious civil war, they might have said it was causing more trouble than it was worth.

There's an obvious analogy there to our love/hate relationship with social media. Giving anyone who could turn on a cell phone access to their own personal media outlet once sounded like a wonderful utopian idea. Maybe it will be, once we all calm down and learn to stop overreacting to every half-baked post or tweet.

Humans seem evolutionarily hard-wired to embrace any new technology that offers a short-term advantage — regardless of how much we dislike the social change it brings. If we were collectively smarter, we might have decided to park the rapid development of AI for a few years while we learned to cope with the social disruption of the internet and social media. It's not like there aren't plenty of other challenges for scientists, such as curing cancer or investigating viruses, or fast-tracking decarbonisation.

We chip away at that stuff but solving these long-standing problems is much less exciting than creating bright, shiny new toys to play with.

I'd blame capitalism — the money follows the path that will make more money — but I think that's just a symptom of our own psychological failing as a species.

If an advantage is available to us individually, we struggle to forgo it for the collective good. It's a problem that is illustrated in the famous example of Game Theory — the Prisoner's Dilemma.

THE PRISONER'S DILEMMA AND GAME THEORY

If you've watched the TV show *Breaking Bad*, you've seen Game Theory in action. Anti-hero Walter White's superpower (apart from his ability to cook meth) is his understanding of the concept. He is able to win high-stakes showdowns with criminal underworld bosses by anticipating patterns of behaviour and applying bold strategies to negate them. For example, when White throws down a bag of explosive mercury in front of local drug lord Tuco in the first season, he is playing on the idea of mutually assured destruction.

Game Theory is a relatively new science of human behaviour, pioneered in the 1920s. It uses mathematical models to try to understand the underlying psychology and economics of human strategy. In other words, how and why we make the decisions we do. Economists have applied it to their thinking about the decisions made by business and government, as well as individuals.

The basis of the theory is to view human interaction like a game, then try to map the logical strategic moves the players are likely to make to try to win that game.

There are numerous hypothetical scenarios that have been studied to better understand how humans behave. One of the most famous is called 'The Prisoner's Dilemma'.

Imagine two individuals, Prisoner A and Prisoner B, are arrested for a crime. The police don't have enough evidence to convict them of a serious crime, but do have enough to convict them on a lesser charge. The prisoners are placed in separate rooms and interrogated. Game Theory maps their options and looks at the most logical choice available to them.

The first possibility is that both prisoners refuse to confess or implicate the other prisoner. In this case, they would both serve a short sentence for the lesser charge.

The second option is that one prisoner remains silent while the other confesses. The one who confesses cuts a better deal and gets a shorter sentence, while the other receives a longer sentence.

The third possibility is that both prisoners confess, meaning they both serve a medium-length sentence.

The dilemma is due to the fact that each prisoner has an incentive to betray the other, in order to get a shorter sentence. But if both prisoners betray each other, they both end up with a longer sentence than if they had remained silent.

The Prisoner's Dilemma highlights the tension between what is rational at an individual level and what is rational collectively. It's a dilemma we face on a grand scale when we consider issues like forgoing cheap polluting energy to help save the planet. Perhaps, though, there is no amount of forewarning about a technology that can stop humans from adopting it. And, boy, were we forewarned about AI.

AI adoption in the office

AI made a great leap into public consciousness with the arrival in 2022 of ChatGPT, a chatbot developed by the OpenAI organisation. Suddenly computers are really talking to us. They can do our homework and write essays and maybe even do our jobs for us.

Not that the use of AI and computer learning is new in the tech sector; it has been driving apps like Uber, and logistics for big online retailers like Amazon, for years. In 2016, research by management consultancy McKinsey & Co. found that 45 per cent of US jobs could be automated by technology that already existed. That percentage is rising all the time. McKinsey updated its estimates in 2023. Where it previously said half of all work will be automated between 2030 and 2075, it now sees us getting to that point by 2060.

But the fact that machines *can* do our jobs doesn't mean they *have* to. And it almost certainly doesn't mean we, or our children, won't have jobs to do. If we're lucky, it might just mean we work fewer hours at less menial tasks. After all, technology has created at least as many jobs as it has replaced.

A 2023 World Economic Forum *Future of Jobs* report offered a strong hint that we were getting carried away with our fears about AI adoption.[22] Its survey found businesses and other organisations estimated that 34 per cent of all business-related tasks are performed by machines, with the remaining 66 per cent performed by humans.

The report noted a shift from the 2020 survey, where the majority of respondents had said they expected almost half (47 per cent) of business tasks would be automated in the following five years. 'Today, respondents have revised down their expectations for future automation to predict that 42 per cent of business tasks will be automated by 2027,' the report concluded. 'Task automation in 2027 is expected to vary from 35 per cent of reasoning and decision-making to 65 per cent of information and data processing.'

That research highlights the point — illustrated by the dot.com crash — that technology often takes longer to change the world than we think it will. For the business sector, adopting new technology involves a great deal of capital outlay — and therefore risk. Early adopters may gain a critical advantage, but they may also run out of money if the gains are not immediate. Most businesses need to borrow for big capital expenditure,

---

22   *The Future of Jobs Report 2023* (digest), World Economic Forum, April 2023, www.weforum.org/reports/the-future-of-jobs-report-2023/digest/.

and that means convincing a bank to take the risk too.

For legacy businesses that already make good money, any revenue gains or cost savings from a new technology can't be marginal to justify taking the extra risk; they need to be clear cut. Businesses are biased towards the proven pathways where they know they can make money. That's why most new tech comes from start-ups, which don't have any existing revenue to lose.

There's still money to be lost, of course, and that's why a specialist investment sector, venture capitalism, has evolved. Venture capitalists have formulae for investing in an array of new technology companies to hedge their bets. Most start-ups fail, but occasionally a Facebook or an Uber will turn an industry upside down — or disrupt it, as corporate people love to say.

Once start-ups get some traction with a new technology, legacy businesses will see that they have to adopt the new tech to compete or risk extinction. They have to make a choice about buying the up-and-coming tech firm or trying to create their own version. Both options are risky, and it's remarkable how tempting it is for businesses to stick to historic revenue paths, even as they dwindle and extinction looms. Can you remember the last time you heard from Kodak or Yellow Pages?

Yes, the march of technology is relentless, but it often gives us more breathing room than we expect. Or it ends up working out in ways that we don't quite expect.

Old jobs, new jobs

New technology can create new jobs, but it also brings change. We increasingly have to be prepared to be flexible about what we do across a lifetime of work. In 2021 a report from McKinsey (again) estimated that one in 16 workers would have to switch occupations by 2030.[23] It

---

23   *The Future of Work After COVID-19*, McKinsey Global Institute, February 2021, www.mckinsey.com/featured-insights/future-of-work/the-future-of-work-after-covid-19.

forecast that job growth would be more concentrated in high-skill jobs like healthcare or science, technology and engineering, while middle- and low-skill jobs (like food service, production work and office support roles) would decline.

An example of a job we can all see disappearing is the supermarket checkout operator. We already increasingly use electronic self-checkout counters. They are a bit annoying and seem to require an assistant to fix something every 10 items or so. But it's not hard to imagine they'll get better and better.

The good news is that it's not most people's dream to be a checkout operator. That kind of work is important for many people, but we are still going to need those people for all sorts of other jobs — because the total workforce is shrinking!

McKinsey identified the job categories that would see more growth than others. The big one was health and age care, given that the world's population is getting older. According to the US Census Bureau, America's median age increased by 0.2 years to 38.9 years between 2021 and 2022. In 1970 it was just 28 years.

In New Zealand the median age is 38. Stats NZ says the number of over-65s in the Kiwi population is expected to hit one million by 2028 (that's around 18 per cent, compared to just 10 per cent in 1980).[24]

Older populations will also be more active than ever before. Many of them will have money and still want to go out and eat and be entertained. They will travel. But yes, we're also going to need a lot of healthcare workers. Not to get too grim about it, but there are already worries about a shortage of undertakers. Are we ready for robots in the funeral home?

Industries like agriculture, forestry and horticulture also desperately need workers. A lot of tasks in those sectors are ripe for more automation. But farming can be messy stuff and there are plenty of primary industry

---

24   'One Million People Aged 65+ by 2028', Stats NZ, 27 July 2022, www.stats.govt.nz/news/one-million-people-aged-65-by-2028/.

jobs that still look a long way from being robot-friendly.

In 2020, the government launched the Agritech Industry Trans-formation Plan to try to accelerate the adoption of new technology in agriculture and horticulture. Its admirable goal is to boost farming productivity, lower carbon emissions and develop the local agritech sector. But a 2021 report by the NZ Institute of Economic Research warned it wasn't going to be simple.

'Investing in capital is generally riskier than investing in migrant labour,' the report concludes. 'Up-front costs can be high, and especially when specialist equipment is involved, decisions are less easily reversed.'[25]

Is the future inflationary or deflationary?

Surely, with all this technology improving things, the cost of living should ease? It certainly hasn't felt that way for the past few years. Nevertheless, the broader long-term trend has been for things to get cheaper. Things that were once luxuries, like chocolate and exotic fruits, have fallen in price relative to incomes and are now a part of everyday life. Electronic devices – from computers to TVs and kitchen appliances – are all much cheaper in relative terms than they were for our parents.

But to work out what the future might deliver us, we have to consider a range of factors, some of which may be pushing in different directions.

In theory, the same demographic forces that are slowing growth – an older population, which is saving more and spending less – will apply disinflationary pressure to the economy. So far, so good. But we also need to consider the costs of caring for older people.

As old Bill Phillips showed us with his curve (see page 82) – and as we saw in the post-pandemic economy – worker shortages add costs to business. Demand for labour pushes up wages, which is good for workers,

25   *Picking cherries: Evidence on the effects of temporary and seasonal migrants on the New Zealand economy*, NZIER report to the New Zealand Productivity Commission, February 2021.

but also pushes up prices. If we don't also get real gains in productivity, then we just end up with high inflation.

Whichever way the long-term trend breaks, there will still be global supply shocks; things like wars, pandemics and climate change will still push up food and supply chain costs and cause inflation spikes. If anything, AI needs to hurry up and get its act together.

Chapter 20

Where next?

We run the country, in many ways, like it's 1975.
— Christopher Luxon*

*(as opposition leader, October 2023)

....

New Zealand needs to face up to some big economic challenges on the horizon. We've been distracted: Covid-19, the cost of living, the wild weather . . . all those inputs have preoccupied the economic thinking of Kiwis in the 2020s. But even the stuff that's been working is in dire need of re-evaluation.

Our economic growth through the first two decades of the century has been flattered by fair winds in the form of high net migration, a dairy boom, a tourism boom and a property boom. I don't mean to dismiss these things as insignificant. The successful marketing of New Zealand as a tourist destination, the productivity gains of our dairy sector and the development of a new export market have been hard won and are worthy of celebrating.

Since we signed a free trade deal with China in 2008 we've seen exports to that country quadruple. As at the start of 2023 they were worth $21.5 billion, comprising $20 billion in goods and $3.4 billion in services. This is a great success when you recall that, at the turn of the millennium, we were largely resigned to the prospect of prices for our food commodity exports being in constant decline. But the revenue paths we've relied on for the past 25 years offer diminishing returns, and that era of rapid export growth is coming to an end. China is maturing as an economy and its demand for our protein is stabilising.

Sure, the leadership in Beijing still has plenty of fiscal firepower to stimulate growth for a while yet, but we can't expect China to keep delivering the same amount of wealth creation. And what happens if tensions with Taiwan escalate to the point that the US demands a trade embargo? We'd be facing the biggest economic crisis in a generation.

It is incredible, and a bit depressing, to consider how little progress New Zealand has made since 1973 when we were stung by the UK entering the European common market. Back then, we relied on meat and wool exports to Britain; here we are, 50 years later, still nervously waiting on the policy decisions of one crucial trading partner.

Or what if the pressures of climate change and advances in technology dramatically accelerate the advance of alternative proteins? It's all very well to scoff at the inability of scientists to re-create prime steak or aged cheese in a lab, but that's not really what our economy is based on. New Zealand sells vast quantities (about 1.6 million metric tonnes a year) of milk powder that is mostly used as a food ingredient. That doesn't seem quite such a difficult thing to replicate cheaply from alternative proteins.

Most of the meat we sell is low-grade beef destined for US hamburgers. Pressure is mounting on consumers to make climate-friendly choices, and plant-based fake-meat burger patties already seem to be on a par with the traditional variety. A tipping point for the economics of these things may be closer than we think.

The upshot of all this is that we need to be working now to create the industries that will drive wealth for the next 50 years. We need to do all those things we looked at to boost productivity, looking at how we educate our kids, investing in R&D, reforming the way our tax system incentivises investment, refining our immigration policies, and building the infrastructure we'll need for our growing population.

The recipe for a more prosperous future New Zealand is right there, and it's not even particularly controversial. If we sit back and wait, then we'll find ourselves back at the dangerous crossroads we reached in the early 1980s. We will limit the choices of the coming generations and force them to head down the same drastic pathways of emergency reform.

There's been no shortage of negativity in the grim aftermath of the pandemic. People are worried about debt and government spending. They are worried about the current account and funding for roads and schools and hospitals. It can sometimes seem like we are in a precarious position.

The future's so bright (I gotta wear shades)

Despite all the challenges, I'm an optimist. We are fortunate that the foundations of this economy remain strong. The reforms of the 1980s and 1990s, painful and radical as they were, have stuck. We remain an open, deregulated economy with a floating dollar that rises and falls in value to signal the level of confidence or concern international markets might have about us.

Powerful rating agencies like S&P, Moody's and Fitch still favour us and seem untroubled by our short- and medium-term capacity to keep managing our debt to the world. We remain a country that people want to move to, with a strong reputation for being fair and equitable and free of corruption.

As to our relationship with technology, bumpy as it is, there's no turning back. While we're worrying about kids cheating on essays, artistic copyright and other concerns (like robot war), AI is also being applied to boring business and manufacturing processes in ways that could be quite good for us.

AI has enormous potential to remove costs and boost productivity. No one makes movies about cyborgs with robotic Austrian accents doing the back-end stuff: 'I'll be back . . . to optimise your supply chain.' That's the kind of technological progress we do want.

AI can analyse the world's power usage and apply efficiencies to reduce our energy bills — with obvious spin-offs for helping the environment. It might be a bit hopeful to bank on it solving climate change — but hey, it may be our best shot.

On balance I think it will be a disinflationary force, maybe even deflationary. It could help us deal with labour shortages and produce more wealth with less hard work. It could deliver the kind of benign economic stability that we enjoyed through the 1990s and early 2000s when widespread computing efficiencies first arrived.

When it actually delivers that stuff is far less certain. Also uncertain is the degree of social disruption the new technology will bring with it. We need to deal with the very real existential threat that extreme inequity can bring.

We need to teach the coming generations to cope with technology and harness it. There's another Alvin Toffler prediction, from 1970, that has not dated at all: 'The illiterate of the twenty-first century will not be those who cannot read or write, but those who cannot learn, unlearn, and relearn.'

AI can tell us many things we need or want to know, but we have to learn the right questions to ask it. The biggest risk around it is assuming that, because it can think creatively for us, we don't need to. My fear around AI isn't that it will be better than humans at making art, writing songs and producing movies. My fear is it will only be *nearly* as good as humans, and yet we'll settle for that because it is cheaper and easier.

So we need to teach the next generation to be flexible and adaptive. We can't predict what job skills our children or grandchildren will require, so let's not bother. Whatever they end up doing, the odds are they'll need to be curious and creative, to problem-solve, to focus and to work hard. It's passion that drives all that stuff, and passion is an emotion, something computers still can't get close to.

For all the problems human emotions cause us, they also give us our edge. They provide the spark that drives us forward – the motivation. When passion fires up our quadrillions of neurons, we pull together combinations of thought that continue to leave computers in the dust.

In a nutshell

A lot of my philosophy on money comes back to Warren Buffett's golden rule: invest in yourself, work on skills that make you exceptional and valuable. Get good at something. Earn some money. Save some of it and keep doing that. Invest it, and over time your wealth will grow.

Obviously, I believe there's a lot of other stuff in this book that is worth knowing but, at its core, personal finance is really just common sense. We call that financial literacy these days, and I'm all for making sure young people have it. I hope this book has brought a bit more of it into the world. But if you put it down and whip out your credit card for a mad, debt-fuelled shopping spree, I don't mind.[26]

The goal of this book is to be engaging, and convince you economics is, too. If you can get interested in money for its own sake, that may help you develop positive behaviours around it. Money is important for survival, security, comfort and freedom. But after all that, there is something else humans crave. Life, when basic needs are met, quickly becomes about finding some deeper meaning and connection in the universe.

Earlier in the book, we mused about the love of money being the root of all evil, but I'm not convinced that poverty enhances our spiritual well-being. Neither was Buddha, for the record, despite the fact he's become a poster child for self-inflicted poverty in Western pop culture. In the ancient *Sigālovāda Sutta* he offers some surprisingly down-to-earth advice on what to do with your money: 'One part should be enjoyed, two parts invested in a business, and the fourth set aside against future misfortunes.' As he saw it, making sound investments helped remove financial stress, putting people in a better position to be generous and spread good karma.

It's wonderfully pragmatic advice. And we need to be more pragmatic about money — individually and as a society. Economics is about choices we make and how we allocate the resources available to us. Of course, there's economics in the routine of daily life — the weekly shop, and mortgage payments — but that stuff is mundane, and economics doesn't have to be.

---

26   Don't do that! Get on a financial literacy website like sorted.org.nz and amaze yourself by putting numbers in a compound interest calculator.

There's economics in psychology, sociology, philosophy and even art. It offers us another way to consider what it is to be human. It's worth finding out about how it all works, just for its own sake. If you do that, there's a good chance some of the practical stuff will rub off on you along the way.

That's what happened to me. Don't let the world of financial and economic jargon get in the way of doing that. That's my advice.

Acknowledgements

I need to first acknowledge all the wonderful economists and financial market experts I've worked with over the years; people who've taken the time to talk to me and whose reports and excellent writing I have absorbed for the past 20 years. New Zealand is well served in the field of economics.

So, thank you to Christina Leung and Peter Wilson at the NZ Institute of Economics, Brad Olsen and Gareth Kiernan at Infometrics, Oliver Hartwich and his team at the NZ Initiative, Sharon Zollner and the team at ANZ, Nick Tuffley and the team at ASB, Jarrod Kerr and his team at KiwiBank, Kelly Eckhold, Michael Gordon, Satish Ranchhod and the team at Westpac, Stephen Toplis and the BNZ team, Paul Bloxham at HSBC, Cameron Bagrie, Ganesh Nana, Dominick Stephens, Shamubeel Eaqub, Professors Robert McCulloch, Tim Hazledine and (sociologist) Paul Spoonley.

Thanks also to the central bankers past and present who took the time to talk me through things — Alan Bollard, Graeme Wheeler, Adrian Orr, Grant Spencer, Christian Hawkesby, Paul Conway, John McDermott and Yuong Ha.

I am grateful also to the many brokers, fund managers and analysts who've taught me how to watch markets: the late Brian Gaynor, Mike Taylor, Matt Goodson, Shane Solly, Paul Glass, Mark Lister and Arthur Lim, Sam Stubbs and many more.

And politicians from the left and the right: Sir Roger Douglas, the late

Sir Michael Cullen, Sir John Key, Sir Bill English and Grant Robertson.

To NZME and my current *NZ Herald* editors Murray Kirkness, Duncan Bridgeman and Tamsyn Parker, thank you for your ongoing support, and to the *NZ Herald*'s Fran O'Sullivan, Shayne Currie, Miriyana Alexander, Tim Murphy and the late Jim Eagles, for backing me at key moments in my career. Garry Sheeran and Greg Ninness, who helped me take off my business journalism training wheels, my thanks to you, too.

A special word to the *Business Herald* team past and present who have fed my enthusiasm for finance and economics. In particular, Grant Bradley, Anne Gibson, Jamie Gray, Mark Fryer, David Rowe, the late Christopher Adams and Brian Fallow (whose economic writing set a standard and the tone I still aspire to).

Thanks to Claire Murdoch at Penguin Random House for challenging me to do this and coaching me through the book-writing process along with Emily Simpson and Stu Lipshaw. I am also very grateful to the following people who took time out of their busy lives to review this book and provide quotes for the cover: former Prime Minister Sir John Key; personal finance writer and seminar presenter, Mary Holm; former Deputy Prime Minister Grant Robertson; Chief Executive and Principal Economist at Infometrics, Brad Olsen; personal finance journalist and educator, Frances Cook; and investigative journalist Guyon Espiner.

And special thanks to all the friends who've talked economics with me at those BBQs and who've supported me throughout my career, especially Guyon Espiner for the ongoing motivation and inspiration. To all the Christchurch old boys, Sam, Whetham, Grant, Tom, Jamie, Stu, Ivan and the rest of the Troubadour Tag Team, and to so many other friends who've listened patiently while I've ranted about this project: Benn and Merrin, the camping collective (where this book was born), Gabe and Kelly, Scott and Libby, John D and Suzie. And to all the rest of the wider Auckland crew: Dave, Alan P, Alan C, Lisa, Trevor, Todd, Alex, Toby, Ed, Dylan, Nigel and Natalie, Winston, Tristram, Jubt, Brooklyn, John P, Tito and all the vinyl lovers of the Rebel Soul and Cupid Bar community.

Finally, to my family: Jenn, Ellie, Theo and Casey; Russell Dann; Corin and Lotta Dann and their children Axel, Kaspar and Jakob; Amy and Joe Evans and their children Ben and Mac — thank you for always being there on the journey.

To Jenny Wilson, the late great Dick Inwood and Andrew Inwood, special thanks for helping me see that I could do this finance stuff, along with all the rest of the Aussie whānau: Rob, Naomi, Spencer, Fraser, Sarah, Megan and the late Roger.

Thanks to James (Ed Musik) Macbeth Dann, Laurie, Lindsay and Geordie, the late Chris Dann, Aaron, Alison and Kirsten, Graeme, Sally, Andrew and Nicole.

To Sue, Dave, James, Ness, Katy, Sam, Kyle and the Hawkes, Fraser, the Laking and Forrester whānau, my thanks for providing a great test market for economic rants at countless BBQs and family gatherings.

And thanks to my grandparents Harry and Phyllis Inwood and Colin and Molly Dann for the values that underpin this book.

Index

About the author

Liam Dann is one of New Zealand's most trusted business and finance journalists, with a writing and reporting career spanning over 25 years.

Currently Business Editor at Large at the *New Zealand Herald*, he delivers insightful, unbiased, accessible opinion and commentary covering markets, economics and politics.

He hosts the podcast *Money Talks* and video show *Market Watch* and regularly appears as a guest commentator across a wide range of media.

From his unlikely origins as a surfer, part-time DJ and self-described bogan, Liam worked in London's banking sector and travelled extensively before evolving into one of New Zealand's most respected commentators. He spends his money on records and sneakers and lives with his family in Auckland.